BARE

Copyright © 2016 Clifton L. Brown

Published by Ibhubesi Books
www.ibhubesibooks.com

Cover Design: C. L. Brown
Cover Art: Dan Graffeo
Author Photo: Jason Cowell

All rights reserved. Printed in the United States of America by Ibhubesi Books. This book may not be reproduced in whole or in part without written permission, except in the case of brief quotations embodied in critical articles and reviews; nor may any part of this book be reproduced, stored in a retrieval system or transmitted in any form by any means, electronic, mechanical, photocopying, recording or other without written permission. For information contact the Publisher at address specified above or visit: www.authorclbrown.com

FIRST EDITION

ISBN: 0-9962013-3-5
ISBN-13: 978-0-9962013-3-9

ALSO BY C. L. BROWN

Loud Whispers of Silent Souls

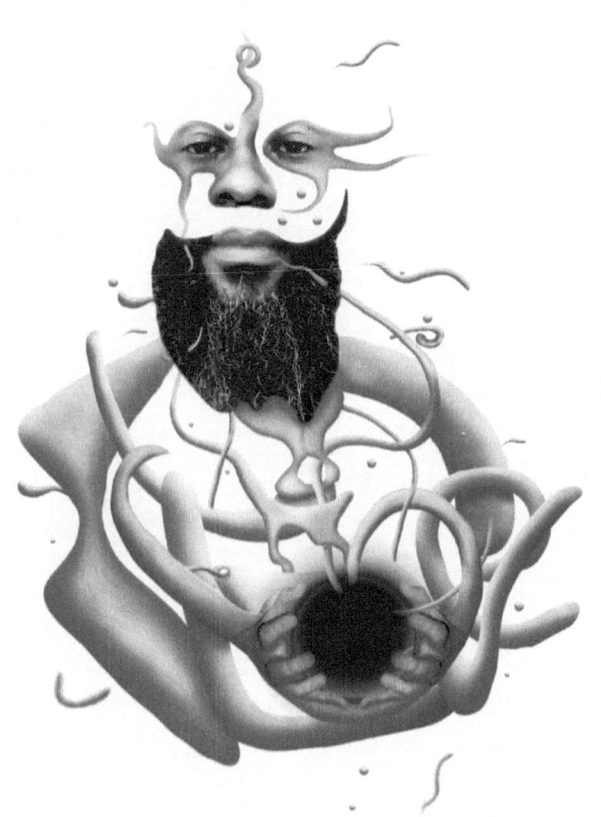

BARE

C. L. Brown

Contents

Thanksgiving	xiii
Acknowledgements	xv
Foreword	xvii
From my Divine Self to Your Divine Self	xix
Why?	2
Endless	5
Replenished	8
Burning Bridges	10
Falling for Forever	13
Skin Deep	15
Runaway	16
In the Cool of the Day	18
You are Beautiful, Self	20
Sound of Silence	22
Song of Broken Strings	24
Eye See	26
Songless	27
Condemned	30
Stay With Me	31
Dreamer	32
Shattered	33
Beneath Your Beautiful	34
One	35
Save Me	36
That Place I Often Am	39

Indecent Proposal	40
Days Like This	45
Reciprocity	48
Cycles	51
Sticks and Stones	53
Priceless	55
Outside of Her	56
Mind Games	57
Fleeting Aspiration	60
Freedom	65
Naked Poem	69
Residue	73
Embrace of Death	75
Specter	76
Crossing (For Keisha... Remembering Jason)	78
Colorful Resentment	82
Soliloquy	85
Songbird (Remembering Dr. Maya Angelou)	90
Praying Hands	92
Wine Tasting	95
Songstress	96
Waiting	100
Procession to Freedom	103
Falling	104
Cosmic Dance	105
Waste	107
Lunacy	111

Sand in the Wind	112
Emptied	114
Addiction	115
Devil	116
Pieces	117
Finders Keepers	119
Broken Chain	120
Wildfire	121
Last Supper	123
Redemption	125
Denouement	127
Release	129
One Mile	130
Unhindered	132
Lipstick Apologies	136
Gone Girl	139
Empty Pages	141
Baggage	144
At the Voice of Love (For Grandma "Mama")	147
You Deserve	150
Recollection	152
Tonight	154
Birth of Transitional Coupling	157
Someone Loves You	159
Goodbye Road	160
Woman of Shame	163
One Man's Trash	164

Sinner	165
Misplaced	168
It's Stranger Inside	171
I Wrote This for You	173
My Beloved	175
Complete Moons, and Star Dusted Skies	177
God's Prettiest Thought	180
Purgatory	182
Former Things	184
Between the Rains	186
Monologue	189
When the World Grows Silent	191
Futile	194
Dust	196
Restoration	199
Open and Shut	201
Soul of Heaven	202
God of Wonders	205
Fear of Fear	207
Shells of Sea's Shore	210
Into the Mystic (Remembering Craigmore & Keroy)	212
Brother's Keeper	214
Her Song, My Love	217
Bare	220

Thanksgiving

I give eternal thanks, and great honor to the One in whom I live, and move, and have my being. To my family, friends, and every single person who has believed in, and encouraged me on this remarkable journey. I am forever grateful!
Thank you!

Acknowledgements

When I was thirsty you gave me drink. Journeys worth undertaking begin and end with the love, and support of those you meet along the way. They are made memorable by the stories of courage, hope, defeat, and triumph you share with those who are willing to listen, and to share. This journey, quite certainly, wouldn't have been as incredible without the following...

My beautiful mother Hyacinth Brown. Sleep in divine peace Mom. My father, Earl Brown, brothers and sisters: Patricia, Michelle, Pamela, Ortnell, Jermaine, Keron, and Dwight. My cousins: Peter, Melody, Wess, Tamar, Tanya, Ricardo, Shedave, Suan, Craigmore, Tarshia, Jackie, and Alenia. My dear friends: Chris, Keisha, Duane, Leon, Roan, Nicola, Danielle, Michelle, Tanya, Elena, Carlos, Jon, Vanessa Rivas, Pablo, Debbie, Jason, Marlon, Vanessa Le-Fook, Lesley-Ann, Joy, and Fallon. I thank each, and every one of you for being a "cup of water" when I needed a drink. A special thanks to the beautiful soul, the amazing Poet, Rebecca "Butterfly" Vaughns. Your kindness, and encouraging words shall forever stay with me. Dr. Dan Graffeo, our conversations are truly a source of inspiration. Thank you for blessing me. To each and every person who has supported, and encouraged me along this journey; everyone who's shared, commented, and liked on Social Media. I thank you all from the core of my being.

Foreword

The beauty of the 26 letters of the alphabet is found in the way they are weaved by souls anointed to be authors. Individuals who pen thoughts that are of fiction, non-fiction, how to scenarios, and poetry. The reader allows for their eyes to indulge in a piece of literary heaven. Every book lover knows that there's nothing sweeter than being able to reference a perfect line, quote, or just share something good with someone.

C.L. Brown is definitely a poet's POET!!! His metaphors are beyond amazing. In the area of love, he gives the reader hope in the essence of something he, or she may have given up on. C.L. Brown writes with an emphasis on letting the woman know her worth, and value. One can surely see themselves in the midst of his words.

In this collection of poems, you'll find yourself on a lyrical ride you don't want to end. I'm into titles, and C.L. Brown was very creative in choosing his. The book title *Bare* alone is quite inviting in itself. My favorite poems are Why?, Songs of Broken Strings(he wrote my life story in this one), Waste, and God's Prettiest Thought(the ultimate dedication poem). Believe me when I tell you that your eyes will thank you for introducing them to the writing style of C.L. Brown!!!

~Rebecca "Butterfly" Vaughns, Author~
Poet/Spoken Word Artist

From my Divine Self to Your Divine Self

You are a stone cut from a great mountain, but although a stone cut, within, you are the essence of the entire mountain. You put to test the strength in the wings of mighty eagles. You prepare the commencement of the river's flow. You are a shield, and a hiding place for the meek. You are a source of strength for the weak. You are the craftsmanship of the Most High; the habitation of the Spirit of God. As a seed planted in purpose, you are here to bear fruit for our world. You are here to make it better than you found it. You are here to declare the glory of the One everlasting.

You are a constant reminder to the inspired that great things are possible to those who believe, and dare take the leap. You must remember that love conquers all, that God is Love, and that you are the image, and the likeness of Love. Hence, there shall be nothing placed before you that you do not possess the capacity to overcome, because love surmounts all things.

This is my blessing over you this day. These words should never leave you. Sow them within the rich soil that is your soul that you may eat of their fruit all of your days. Let them remind you when doubt starts whispering sweetly into your spirit. Let them keep you when deep hunger sets in at the adversary's table while others partake in the feast of stones.

Sometimes you have to become nothing before
you can blossom into something.

BARE

Bare

> I swear God took a little more time with you. Whether perfecting his finesse, or simply relishing His art, I do not know. I just know He was with you for a good while longer than most.

C. L. Brown

Why?

I asked the wind
Yes, the wind
It said, "Receive me into your soul"
It is then I was bewitched by your scent,
    now I can't breathe without you anymore
I asked the trees, and they mimicked
    through dance the freedom I saw once
    in the gracefulness of your touch
Now I sit in the concert of countless leaves
    hoping to relive you just once more
I asked the stars,
    they said, "We are ashamed
    each night she opens those eyes"
I asked the moon,
    and she spoke of the blessing she was given
    each night she made her soul
    to freely roam upon your skin
I asked the sun
He said, "I might as well flee into the night,
    because the morning she rose in your sight
    was the last time you looked to me for light"
I ask the birds,
    they danced, and sang the most winsome song
    when they remembered your beauty,
    your grace,
    your elegance
I asked the Honeybee
He said, "You know, if only my honey
    was as sweet as she"
I asked the butterfly
She said, "Her spirit bears a freedom
    that is the envy of my wings;
    now I desire only to fly in the gleeful streams
    of her vibrant thoughts"
I asked the clouds

Bare

They said, "O yes! We adore the melting
    of our souls upon her covering"
Now I lay beneath countless droplets of the rain
    hoping you'll saturate me once again
I asked the river
She boasted of her sensual curves
    carved as she meandered
    through your flawless figure
I asked the White Lotus,
    purely gorgeous her flower
She said, "I am but a whisper
    of the splendor she has to offer"
I asked the fire
He begged for a sip of water
Said he sparked inside your soul,
    and found his flames in complete danger

So you see my Darling,
I've inquired of everything,
    and they've all said the same thing
You are the epitome of God's perfection
And that is why, I love you
And even when time reaches a time
    when she needs more time,
    even then,
    I will still be in love
    with every single thing about you

C. L. Brown

> I write what I see, what I feel; both in the natural, and the spiritual. The credit then must be given to the subject, because I'm only an interpreter trying to tell the world what it is trying to say.

Bare

Endless

I AM the endless love you were conceived of
Eternal, and beautiful
The kind like water cradled in the sands of the Sahara
Inimitable, and precious
Loving you with a passion
    that burns like wildfire
    consuming domestic possessions
Passing through,
    and around you,
    finding my being in the care
    of hands fashioned with purpose
And Sweetheart, the things I see making passes
    below your surface
My God!
I am too selfish to speak of them
But somehow, I manage to give away bits
    when I am the recipient of my heart's
    whispered secrets
Darling, of all the sweet things acquainted
    with my lips, you are unparalleled
So, like the Honeybee patiently searching
    for that perfectly saccharine Sunflower,
    I'll impart unrushed kisses inch-by-inch
    until every mystery hidden in your skin
    tastes familiar
With those gorgeous freckles
    accentuating your flawless,
    you are the reflection of stars
    God stitched into the very soul of the heavens
And you are perfect,
    something like cloudless fall skies
    when shades of blue and light greys meet in
    one place cradling the partially woken moon
    when east suns fall short of mid-skies,
    only infinitely more wonderful

C. L. Brown

So, in awe of our perpetual unfolding,
    I anxiously linger in the expanse of your eyes,
    because that's where I feel most free
And when I'm there,
    I slow my breathing,
    cheating time,
    or at least I try
Darling, I am incessantly in love with the muted
    conversations of your fingers familiarizing
    themselves with my excited skin,
    because you reveal emotions buried within
    each time they pass against me
And I am in love with the totality of your being,
    because when fear found a place
    inside the inner self,
    and my lips fixed themselves
    to speak into existence our nonexistence
You knew just how to speak life into my spirit,
    and as the redeemed,
    we were born again
Darling beyond a lover, you are my friend
And if in death God should ask me to live again
I would sin again
With you again
Making love a lifetime
Just to die again
Then repeat you
Then repeat you
And then repeat you
All over, again

Bare

> She asked why I always speak so poetically. I smiled, took a picture, and showed her my inspiration. For the first time she understood my perspective, and it worked, because now she inspires me a million times more.

C. L. Brown

Replenished

She was colors of beautiful
    painted across his pitch-black soul
She was a message from God
A reminder he'd already seen the worst

Though he only saw her those one hundred days,
    she pulled sacred waters
    from his abandoned well
She gave him purpose again
Her colors were brightest then
    when hope found a place in the heart
    of an expiring man

She is colors of beautiful
    painted across his pitch-black soul
She is a message from God
He's now back at his worst
Smiling with her ghost
That old familiar Hell

Bare

Some days I loan my eyes to the shell that keeps you away from me. I often read curiosity in your eyes as you wonder what it is I see in you. Sometimes your insecurity is quite evident. But rest your worries Darling, for when I lend my eyes to your skin, I'm simply trying to fathom how amazingly beautiful your soul must be.

C. L. Brown

Burning Bridges

She lit an angry flame in the pile of disappointments,
    exasperating it with resentments;
        burning worn-out bridges to old memories,
        because I was no longer home
But there I stood the fool
    trying to rebuild the road to familiar comfort
    from the vestiges of broken promises

I was begging her to stay, in fear
She was walking away, in freedom
Then I thanked God it was all a dream
    as I dried the pillow
    where my eyes witnessed the ordeal
Those runaway tears broke covenant with my heart
    revealing lies I'd buried inside foolish pride
My undying love for love was the breath
    trapped inside her lungs
But she was tired
So she exhaled waiting those unfruitful years
Now death enquires about the vacancy
    she left within me,
    and seven-fold the misery has taken residence

You see, she was my savior
The one standing between myself,
    and the pit where hordes of self-destructive
    thoughts awaited my devolution
    to self-gratifying acts of sin
Now I'm here,
    burning with those bridges,
    anchored in broken promises
    trying to convince her otherwise
It wasn't supposed to be this way,
    but I did once promise I'd love her
    beyond this flesh

Bare

How humbling reciting such things
    in this transition
My eye had adjusted to her Light
Now I'm feeling my way through this darkness,
    guided by the remains of the fire
    that consumed those bridges,
        finding my way back to vacant memories

C. L. Brown

> Sometimes I wish to spend the remainder
> of what I have left inside the womb of
> darkness, but then I think of her.
> She gives me reason.
> So I rise.

Bare

Falling for Forever

Be still my escape
Be as patient as unhurried clouds
    casting shadows over the calm of turquoise waters
Just one steady breath each time
Take me slowly in
Hold me in until I perfuse absolutely everything
    that is you
Allow me to spend time inhaling the excess wind
    taking recess from your skin
Oh!
My Darling!
I imagine the mist from the deep was as pure
    in the genesis of everything
As pure as the feel of your fingers
    finding a place between mine
As pure as the feeling I get when both
    your body, and your soul
    find rest in these loving arms of mine

Be still, my forever
Take no care for tomorrow
For I AM your today
Here today
To ensure forever,
    love will always be very well acquainted
    with even the air taking precious secrets
    from your Secret

You see God, my Darling, is well pleased
    having perfected his hands the moment
    he fashioned you,
    taking thought of my most essential need
I take myself into your eyes,
    and it is quite evident where it was
    God mastered the stars

C. L. Brown

Why it was angels forsook forever
Why it is I am falling forever

So please, suspend your soul inside my own
Make me your home
And I will see to it a day never dies
    having not witnessed my lips giving devotion
    to the aura encasing your inviting covering
I bask myself in the amalgamation of words
    and tones leaving your lips,
    and witnessed the dove's wings shaping
    the still midmorning wind
Darling, God has yet made anything as tranquil
    as the sound of the air escaping your soul

So I search you
Deeply!
I forget to supply my lungs, watching the opening,
    and closing of the gates the restless seek
    in their ultimate day
And to think, all of me was created to love all of you
And to think, all of you was created
    to put together the scattered pieces
    of the mystery that is God

I see divinity inside of you
I comprehend those things
    sacred spirits are trusted with
I hear the chirping of bluebirds,
    and dance with the majestic souls
    of towering trees
All because of you
And as much as I grow anxious
    to pass time inside your mind,
    I am reluctant to start,
    because forever is simply not enough,
    to love someone as amazingly gorgeous, as you

Bare

Skin Deep

The way the lukewarm water
    clung to her skin
I saw glimpses of her soul with
    each flash of the lightning
And with her nipples rising
    and my tongue relishing her breasts,
        she pulled at my desires
            until I had nothing left
I was dining on her neck
She was sniffing the air
    searching for a breath
    as my fingers searched out the spot
    for which I was erect
I was biting on her flesh
    as she climbed up
        then slowly showed me her depths
I was so impressed
So I pressed
Then I felt her arms
    tightening around my neck
Inside and out she was completely wet,
    leaving me
        completely thirsty
So without a hurry,
    in a candlelit tub,
    mind slowed,
    sipping White Hennessey;
    I submerged my totality into her
    divine energy,
    licking the sweet residue
    of her satisfied soul

C. L. Brown

Runaway

This morning I cloaked myself
    in the ocean's serenade
I needed to know if a piece of our last time
    remained behind
I was regurgitating madness,
    pounding the sand with my fists
Wiping the salty tears saturating my lips
But the ocean
She heard me
Sent her waters to console me
They washed away your memory
Then I watched her waters being pulled away slowly
The same way you took your love
I was hurting bad
For the first time since we met, I was truly sad
So I looked up in search of God
I needed answers,
    but God,
    like your voice inside my head,
    was completely silent
So I looked to the sun as it slowly rose
It reminded me of that fire you had in your eyes
    the way it burned my skin
Had me thinking of the inferno I felt
    inside of you each time you drew me in
Then I thought how that scene was so fitting
Because with you I laid so many rainy days in sin,
    but there I was in the depths of the water's soul
    as Jesus on that day John immersed Him
But this poem I didn't write for you
    will be the last thing
So read one last time,
    and know you're no longer my everything
My runaway Darling

Dare

> Her lips are my favorite place in this entire world. When I go there, I rarely speak, but from my soul, I listen very well.

C. L. Brown

In the Cool of the Day

It is quite evident that God discovered overtime
    when He placed his fingers into the void
    that was masterfully molded
    into her enticing smile

To be quite honest,
    I heard her name when a song seeped through my
    porous soul, and something sweetly whispered
    when I was told,
    "God knows rest where the
    Honeybee wishes to play"
I was completely perplexed by the vague nature
    of the statement,
    but I wasted no time in my pursuit

We spoke the language of poetry,
    conversing in our purified forms
    as our tongues took great pleasure
    tasting each other,
    and our fingers found purpose
    stirring a little trouble
I exercised perfect patience in her coming,
    laying bare myself in the cool of her stay

At the end of the day,
    she walked away with teeth marks trailing
    from her lips down past her chin
I walked away with lipstick stains
    masking my coffee-colored face,
    listening to the ocean's waves tip-tapping
    away on loosed grains of wet sand

Needless to say, I was thoroughly satisfied,
    though I couldn't help wondering where next
    the clues will leave me breathless

Bare

> Love God with all of yourself. Love your neighbor as you do yourself. In other words, love yourself so that you can give your all to God, and love yourself so you will learn how to love your neighbor.
> Just love yourself!
> Period!

C. L. Brown

You are Beautiful, Self

In the calm of that night,
    amidst the clamorous congregation
    of fervent emotions,
    that old guitar sang her heart out to me
    dispelling notions of my eternal damnation
She said I needed saving,
    and love she played on those worn out strings
    conveying me to the arms of a comfort
    I couldn't comprehend

In the calm of that night,
    a Rose bloomed outside the reach of her sun,
    and gracious she was opening her eye
    commencing my understanding

In the calm of that night,
    a tiny bird passed time perched in the
    giant Sycamore manning the window
    through which my spirit flew
She told me things that made the man in
    the mirror a complete stranger
And I should tell you,
    God has no definition for man to compose
So to Him be all glory
For it was the first time in a good time
    since I'd seen myself

Bare

> You don't need people to validate you. God validated you the day He created you. What you are here for, and who you are has nothing to do with the opinions of others, so stop trying to find your place in them.

C. L. Brown

Sound of Silence

Is it OK if I think of you while I pray?
First for you when I open my eyes,
    last for you before I close them?
If I ask God to send his strongest angel
    your way, is that OK?
Do you mind if I completely lose track of time
    while with you?
If I keep reaching for your hand
    until you become my forever?
Is it OK if beautiful sunrises don't fancy me
    those days you will find your rise in my arms?
Is it OK if I live in your amazing smile
    having these crazy feelings in my gut
    I wish not to shake?
Is it OK if I leave your fingers' prints
    etched into my skin?
If you evoke emotions I never felt,
    and I get lost in all the colors of the most
    beautiful eyes I've ever seen,
    are you OK with that?
Is it OK with you if I lose all memory
    of everyone that ever came
    before you said "Hello!"?

I want you to know that I think of you,
    every single day
I write my sadness, not having you
I write my peace,
    you placing tender lips between my eyes
I think of the moon keeping vigil over you
    as you play in the colors
    of dreams that make you forget to breathe
I imagine the taste of the words
    fleeing the abundance of your gorgeous heart
I wonder if someday you will read this,

Bare

    and know that somewhere out here
    is a man who thinks more about your soul
    than he does his own

I wonder if tonight you are afraid,
    maybe alone
I wonder if tears are anywhere near those eyes
I wonder if you need a friend
Someone just to sit, and listen
Because I'd do anything to wrap my arms
    around you, even just one second

Last night I heard raindrops
    falling against thoughts I held of you,
    but I asked them to go to you instead
To sing over you while you lay in bed
You should know I wish to love you
    without a thought of an end
And these words keep floating through my head
So I will think of you until my thoughts,
    and purpose become intimate,
    and you become the one
    I'll die spending time with,
    if that's OK with you

C. L. Brown

Song of Broken Strings

Have you seen the silent fall of aging leaves
    at the whisper of the gentle breeze?
God's most perfect work
How everything begins with the earth,
    and my skin is the color of her dirt
The songs of canary chicks permeate the souls
    of the lovers of all things beautiful
This grand illusion
    seemingly necessary for salvation,
    but it's in her that I found my start,
    and my destination
And the key to this life
    is there in the essence of her kiss
Those gorgeous lips...
I love...
How my fingers pass just above her eyes
    removing the loose strands of fear
    that endeavor to hide
    what my eyes desire most
The sight of her smile
    when love is the voice
    whispering in her sacred place
This perfect work of God;
    hidden there in the quiet of the eyes
    that steal my attention every single time

But she's unfamiliar
Still, I'm trying to capture
    the sound of her laughter
    playing in the wind;
    while in the backdrop
    the songs of canary chicks
    hushed the deluge of words
    that sought a place upon my lips
She's so beautiful in the

Bare

    conversation of unspoken words
And the silent fall of aging leaves
    at the whisper of the gentle breeze
    pales in comparison to her silence;
    when her eyes convey everything
    my wilting heart longs for
This perfect work of God
Hidden there in the Song my broken strings
    are yearning to play

C. L. Brown

Eye See

Eye in one second see everything
    he in a million years could never,
    but words are never enough
    so I never say too much
Besides the wise keep still lips, and listening ears
And thus I've vacated my heart,
    and gathered of those things that fled your soul
        when your love was dying to be heard

Eye love the texture of your complexion
    when the sun expresses passion
        upon your molten brown sugar-like skin
When you become my air,
    and Eye see one more reason
        to stay here

Eye have seen a thousand,
    yet it remains,
        you are the one holding the key to my chains
Yet it remains,
    he is the one sharing the sacred space
        inside the eyes Eye spent former days

Bare

> I am fascinated by this heart of mine, born so free, yet finds such pleasure being a slave.

C. L. Brown

Songless

I used to sing odes to the birth of stars
Having found you at supernova
When death found life in this cyclic spin
When yours was the soul mine fought to win

I remember finding you face down
    on his floor
Then remembered I the miracle
    of that seed planted
Death his eyes beheld,
    but life you were to me
The axe to my Willow Tree
So I hid you in that place the sun never sees
    until your roots anchored inside a love
    destined to supply all your needs

I was in deepest solitude that night,
    my mind completely nude
Wandering in confusion,
    but you opened your eyes allowing me to see
But then you closed them,
    so now I don't sing anymore

Bare

When we live in a Universe that is ever expanding, it is illogical to me that I should ever try fitting into a box. We are as much a part of the Universe as we are of each other. So, if she's expanding, so should we.

C. L. Brown

Condemned

She's arrayed in an inferno
A devil's playground
She opened her mouth, and ambers ignited
    the thoughts I held to dowse her with
But it is said her fire is purifying
So I made bare my skin as Adam on the eve of sin,
    and I dove in,
    completely submitting everything I was
    before the encounter that left me needing
    to be atoned for
She consumed me,
    all except the reasons I am destined never
    to find my place in Heaven
Now I'm dying
Slowly burning
Reenacting the falling of the sons of grace

Bare

Stay With Me

Don't rush
My composed fingers
    slowly excavating the sweet things
    God hid beneath your skin

Don't rush
My admiration
    of the Creator's prowess at mastering colors
    and curves where time,
    and space intersects in your depths

Don't rush
My lips searching the fissures of your flesh,
    immersed in your divine river
    as I drift lifelessly into the nucleus
    of your immaterial existence

Don't rush
The resuscitation of the man fading outside
    the reach of the medicinal words
    perched upon your lips
    as I inhale the ethereal being
    rising from your disembodied self;

My Darling
Don't rush

C. L. Brown

Dreamer

This window holds my freedom
But fear
To be wrapped inside your arms my Dear
As yesterday,
    when your voice soothed me
    like the midnight rain
But this pain
My heart desires you again
But these lips refrain
Resisting these thoughts in my brain

And sleep brings no peace
    when you come to my dreams,
    and I embrace subconscious illusions
Do you go to the moon as I do?
Do you wish upon midnight stars
    as I did once in your eyes?
Your eyes!
How I miss them searching my susceptible soul
    in the thick darkness
    as we stole time in a song,
    and my chest warmed your naked breasts
The beauty of such memory I wish to forget,
    but loyalty is intimate with my heart,
    and thus...
As the moon awaits the falling of the sun,
    I'm still here,
    waiting for you

Bare

Shattered

When I couldn't retain anymore the pain
    of loving her as she walked away
I stood alone in the rain
Saturating myself in a cloudburst
    of sad memories
I was shattered that day
Situated on my knees,
    but couldn't pray
I sunk my fingers into my chest
    aspiring to cease my shallow breathing
Screaming "I love you!"
But the sounds refused to leave
    the heart breaking beneath the weight
    of her absence
Cold tears streaming down my face
I only wanted one more kiss,
    but it seemed my presence she didn't miss
Flicking her wrist like I meant nothing
Funny how to me, she's still everything

C. L. Brown

Beneath Your Beautiful

Beneath your beautiful where I haven't seen
A smile breaks your lips
    while this glass of brown rum I sip
Finding God in your eyes where I was to be alone
Even the lines etched into your skin
    give me reason to love you outside our season
Sitting beside you
Without you
Dreaming

That windswept night was our start
When your eyes confused everything my
    flesh, and my soul
    conspired to steal your precious heart
I've spent time conversing with time
Telling her about the sweet things she's yet to see
Suns rising to find you inside of me
Lost inside your windows
    where my soul loves to play
And you are the best of what's left
Though we haven't even met
But my mind told my heart, "Don't fret"
Because good things come to those...
And I'm the one waiting
Dreaming beneath your beautiful,
    where eyes haven't seen

Bare

One

My!
Your skin!
So tempting!
You've got me thinking something of the kind
    that makes me question
        the origin of stars
I love the way you move through my thoughts
    creating ripples in my calm
Pervading my being,
    and you feel so much like home
Your vibration is no strange thing
In fact, it is the melody I was created to sing
So I capture with my poetry the intricacies of your art
Speaking words invading your heart
Because we are the dawn of us
Rising from old dust, and mistrust
Pouring forth trust
    as I thrust my essence
        inside your divine cradle of life,
            where the two that we were
                became the One song
Serenading the One self
The One fruit of pure love

C. L. Brown

Save Me

Her lips touching mine don't beget my eyes to hide
In actuality, they feel peculiar against my skin
I pull her in like vapor,
    allowing her to suffuse the metaphysical nature
    of all that I be,
    but she's unfamiliar
She's tried, but she hasn't supplied valid reasons
    to snare her essence on paper
Not the way you used to
Her smile is your frown I keep losing myself in
    trying to find you
Because her fingers don't read me
    the way yours used to

There is no magic in her eyes to enthrall me
So I make no wishes when I'm inside of them
Her tongue cannot interpret the symbology of pain
    I've written in the depths
    where courage finds purpose
So outward I keep smiling
Forcing my heart to call her Darling
But within,
    without you,
        I'm slowly becoming empty

But I'm trying to hold my composure,
    composing romantic thoughts for the day
    she'll toss me to the pile for you to find
But until then...
I go to sleep every night thinking
    how I'll make us right
Strategizing how I'll rewrite the script
    adding a fresh start to the end of this book
Because when the moon forgot to rise
    you kept my demons within the shadows

Bare

    I'm forbidden to play
Now the day, and the night
    share the same pitch-black face
And I am the playground darkness comes
    to shed its burdens

C. L. Brown

> Perhaps it was the playful nature of the wind, not malicious intent, that gifted the budding rose to the scorching earth.

Bare

That Place I Often Am

There is a place I often am
Lonely
Sometimes broken
Where my thoughts construct
    the very follicles of her skin,
    and my fingers explore my madness
Where fabricated smiles hide my dark secrets,
    and oceans are the words she's spoken
Where I am submerged in the fear
    that is the selfsame breath I need to live
Where I love her in my nothingness, completely;
    though my being is the turbulent wind
    she seeks shelter from

I used to fear the closing of my eyes
    though the moon promised her light
Then in the depths of my solitude,
    she came, and took me away from myself
I've seen death entombed inside her absence
That solitary tree
    dancing in the hidden breeze
    just outside my window
He's so beautiful
And he's there
In that place I often am
Lonely
Sometimes broken
Where oceans are the words she's spoken,
    and I am immersed in her death
Foolishly seeking life

C. L. Brown

Indecent Proposal

Flame-casted silhouettes chronicled our secrets
    like cave paintings
    as our souls danced slowly,
    etching memories on naked walls
And like silk-smooth acoustic melodies
There was a song in her soul that
    gracefully placed my mind at ease
See, I was somewhere,
    lost inside everything about her
Thinking
Wondering how on earth
    God fashioned from past hurts,
    this beautiful key to my prison
See I propositioned,
    and she assumed the position
    while the meddling moon lit my path
    through her sensual curves,
    and I infused the very follicles in her covering
Then I requisitioned,
    "Darling don't you move
    till we reach our destination,
    for I will empty myself
    releasing your frustrations"

Receiving my request her skin beaded with sweat
    as her nipples perked up atop her breasts
Then as my teeth began leaving bite marks
    on the outside of her inner thighs
    her cheeks nervously squirmed,
    crumpling the pearl-white sheets
You see my thoughts were her freedom,
    eliciting emotions she couldn't fathom
So I spoke them,
    manifesting the woman I was craving,
    lying between her untainted truth feasting,

Bare

    savoring the sweet melanin in her skin
Savoring the sweet nectar-like secretions
    of her flower
    as my tongue took lashes at her flesh,
    atoning for her sin,
    for the wages is death

Reaching for her depths
    I tasted death through visions of her afterlife
Reading her skin like braille
    in the absence of bedroom lights
And with my teeth sunk into her breast,
    briefly, I lost my breath
    as she recessed her French-tipped nails
    deep into my chest
Then I closed my eyes wishing
    as she sat gasping,
    fighting to release her last breath

She began biting on my neck
    as the candles' flames
    danced in the subtle wind
    leaving the fan blades;
    dispersing therapeutic earth-like scents,
    intensifying our senses
My soul began pulsating through my piece
    finding peace in the celestial sweets
    concealed in those crumpled sheets
My lips then took pilgrimage from her chest
    passing her neck
    until I released bottled fears,
    nibbling on her ear
But I could no longer bear the thought
    of such shallow existence,
    having tasted loneliness inside her depths
So I emptied myself into her deep blue,
    until I saw her soul

C. L. Brown

Then I sat my tongue beneath her fountain
Drinking truth
Quenching thirst
Then I invaded her as a blind man
    for the first time
    finding purpose in his eyes
Searching her skin in the thick darkness
    infused by the lights of the eyes
    that keep watch of the nights
O how my wishing star gleamed
    that divinely inspired night
    as I sipped from the stream her essence flowed,
    imparting life

See that night I had sins
    trapped inside my skin
    still unforgiven,
    but she was the resurrection
    of my hell-bound soul
She was the fire that held my pardon,
    and though burning,
        I repeated everything I promised not to do again
Because I craved her poison
That feel of the slow creep as when
    death finds his victim
Reflecting on her caramel skin I got lost in this poem
Finding my prison
These words digging her,
    my tunnel to freedom

But that night I remember watching my fingers
    scratching at her skin
    as if the cold grip of hunger was setting in,
    and all I had to eat was there before me,
    entangled in satin sheets,
    buried deep inside the soul of the woman
    I wanted to eat

Bare

That place I found life
There inside her,
    one blissfully passionate night
That night I gave thanks to the Keeper of everything
    that she opened up to let me in
Allowing my fingers to bring forth her glory
    while thoughts I whispered pervaded her soul
    like demons finding victims in deep sleep
See my lustful mind was a womb
    of unconceived desires
So as I penetrated,
    she gave birth,
    and I was born again
I said as I penetrated,
    she gave birth,
    and I was born again

But though my position gave me dominion
    still I asked her permission
    to finish the mission when I begged her,
    "Please Darling!
    don't you fight,
    because it is only right,
    that I eat you this night"

And there I was that night among nights
In the position envied of all positions
With my indecent proposal
Among my darkest thoughts
Professing light
Perfecting my image of the very best her
With love on my lips, poised, ready to spit
With passion in my tongue,
    eyeballing her slit

You see at first she pretended like she didn't,
    but her quaking body told her secrets,

C. L. Brown

    how desperately she needed it
So, patiently I waited for her soul to come
And as I broke the veil to her most holy,
    she spoke slowly
    but screamed loudly,
    and squeezed tightly
    as she held me,
    and I multiplied myself inside her body;
    violently vibrating as my soul gave her everything,
    and that was when,
    she gave birth,
    to the very best me

Bare

Days Like This

I used to think of you on days like this
Days when the rain sings like acoustic instruments
    clutched in the hands of heartbroken musicians
    weeping in candlelit cafés
Where smoke fills lungs,
    aged rum slurs speech,
    and thoughts of sweaty sex pervades
    the minds of young lovers
Where sexual desires drip from untouched women
    inside the arms of determined men
Yes, I used to think of you, on days like this

Days when my skin feels a strange thing
Leaving me craving for your hands
    to remind me that I'm worth something
Days when you licked me like an unfed Lion
    prepping his feast
When just the thought of you leaving my side
    made you want to come again
    when you haven't even left
Days when you held me so tightly I couldn't breathe,
    though the soul has no need
    for the wastes of trees,
    but you made me feel so alive
    when you read naked thoughts through my eyes

Now I sit still in the concert of my own hands
    having their way with me
How gently they touch me
Slowly passing over erected nipples
Covering my lips
Hushing my screams
    when I think of the days your tongue refused
    to stay behind your lips

C. L. Brown

Days when your eyes traced my face
    reading the tiny quivers in my nervous skin
    while my hips submitted to your fingers' tips,
    and my nipples rose revealing
    carefully hidden secrets
Yes, I used to think of you, on days like this

Days when your tongue seemed fused with my flesh,
    and I strained my neck lost in the melody of
    your music bouncing with every trust
    in your waistline
Sipping on exotic red wine as my mind
    slowed your motion
Counting each tick of the clock watching time
    hoping this thrill is not subjected to it
Yes, I used to think of you, on days like this

Days when I left teeth marks on my lips
    grabbing tighter at the sheets
    trying not to lose my grip
Days when you pinned me by my wrists anxiously
    taking everything I have already given
    as though it was your first, and last time
    inside my body, soul and my filthy mind
Oh yes!
I used to think of you, on days like this

Bare

> One act of kindness is more powerful than a million words spoken.

C. L. Brown

Reciprocity

She needed something heavenly
So I wrapped my heart around her soul,
    and loved her deeply
Then calmly I pressed my skin firmly
    against her unclothed body
I felt emotions emerging
    from my immense silence
        where they laid submerged in cold darkness;
    that place monsters play
Her essence was the word God chose
    when he spoke over my emptiness,
        and light came as she washed her rays of grace
        over the cold stone that laid beneath my chest

I needed something earthly to remind me
I needed her beginning to be my end
So like smoke from violent flames
    pervading passing clouds,
    I rose to her heavens,
    and infused her eternity
I lose all balance
    when I view existence through her eyes
Cause all I see is love
How she touches me
How she holds me
How she consoles me
And speaking things others failed to say,
    she uplifts me

The salt of her skin was a necessary thing
    in the recipe we concocted
Dining on the raw taste of flesh has never
    satisfied more eager souls
In the end she hung in my arms
    like a towel waiting for the sun

Bare

   beneath weeping clouds
And I made certain not one drip of her residue
   fell, quenching the lust of the half-filled tub

C. L. Brown

> Have you ever had a glass fall from your hands, and break on the floor? Have you ever tried putting it back together exactly how it was? Nearly impossible, isn't it?
> Some pieces you may never find, and should you keep breaking it over and over again, you will keep losing pieces until that one day when you realize you have nothing left to work with. This is exactly what you are allowing to happen each time you permit someone to break you. Sure, they will try putting you back together each time, but you are never the same. So, break that cycle while you still have enough of you left to recognize yourself.

Bare

Cycles

Why can't I love you the way I promised?
I always swear to do better,
    but only give you better
    until the routine becomes familiar
Then it's back to speaking words to force your heart
    when your mind wants no part of me
I compelled you to pour out your trust
    like the last shot of Glen Silver's Scotch,
    and I sipped it down like an old drunk
    seeking his next fix
But then I got sober,
    and you stood there,
    tears streaming down your face,
    asking, "Will this ever end?"

I grew sad when you threatened to leave
    asking me to change
        then I wrote about it,
            asking you to stay,
                again,
                    knowing damn well
                        I'd remain the same

C. L. Brown

> The forest will intimidate the match until it is struck against a stone.

Bare

Sticks and Stones

Time keeps perfect memory
Words hold no regard for hearts
They cannot understand
They do not differentiate
But they make a home of time's memory
Always there to remind you
    the ego will break anything to fix itself,
    including itself

You see words fell from the lips
    that once spoke her healing
And her heart was lightning struck sand
    falling through my hands,
        breaking promises I swore to the heavens
        forever I'd keep
I prayed nightly losing peace
    tossing in cold sheets
Replaying in my mind her reluctance
    to show me that she felt weak,
        until tears flooded her eyes
        compelling her to release

C. L. Brown

> Through love I learned how to break hearts. Through heartbreak I understood the gift of being loved. I have seen both sides of the coin, and though love requires one to be at risk for heartbreak, I would love a thousand times more, if God grants me a thousand more lifetimes. Because love, she's worth it.

Priceless

You broke me
You spilled my priceless oil,
    and poured my beautiful fragrance
    beneath your feet
I gave you everything
I gave you access to places
    I myself was afraid of entering
All because you said you loved me

Your words were the keys
    I hid in childhood dreams
    when I said one day you would find me
Then you found me,
    and you wooed me
But then you broke me
You spilled my precious fragrance,
    and smeared my oil beneath your vagrant feet

C. L. Brown

Outside of Her

The most beautiful of expressions
    she found there in his presence
        when his lips told her soul
            his heart wanted everything
Because as though it were God in the dawn
    of His beloved garden,
    he spoke over her,
    setting her free from old burdens
He cultivated her with hands
    that understood the fertile nature of ashes
Loving her from the remains of his broken endeavors
Loving her far more than she'd ever imagined
Loving her until he realized outside of her,
    lies nothing

Bare

Mind Games

The slow fall of snowflakes
    finding equilibrium against my skin
Like the cold fingers loneliness brings
I exhaled my last thoughts of you,
    and saw the gray shade of cold air
    rising from our extinguished flame
I've heard silence that would drive fear
    in the hearts of those
    who's taken lives without reason
Trying to quiet my mind through fruitless chatter,
    I convinced myself I was better without you
But at night I can't sleep
Seven days now I haven't digested anything
    except visions of his hands
    occupying your skin
Even went to sleep, and caught a dream about it
Rose up screaming
It was 4:30 in the morning,
    and I swore I'd received the punishment
    of this life of sin,
    because Darling,
    I was burning
Caught a flash, like lightning,
    the image of your lips against my neck,
    and my fingers creeping towards your breast
Then I searched what little light remained in my mind
But I couldn't find you
But I found death,
    sucking the life from this broken heart
    getting cold inside my chest
I don't even know what's next
But I know it won't be my best if I taste her,
    and they're not your lips
No, not those you speak with
Dripping like ink from the pen

C. L. Brown

    interpreting this poem
Red like the blood I'm losing
    carving, cutting, and slicing
    every part of me that smells, resembles,
    and tastes like you;
    every part that reminds me that once
    there was a me and you
I feel like such a fool
    for allowing you to slip through my fingers
    like water in babies' hands
I thought death was freedom
But even in Hell I realized the fire was you
I know maybe I sound a little crazy
But Baby my life got so damn hazy the day I left you

Bare

> When I had no fruit, they said I had no purpose. They didn't understand the concept of seasons. Now they live beneath my branches.

C. L. Brown

Fleeting Aspiration

I'm afraid to show the world the aftermath
    of the night you decided daylight wouldn't
    find you in my life
I can still taste the bitter words departing
    your forked tongue that mangled the man
    you were supposed to mend
I'm afraid to show those walls
    I wrote infinite versions
    of our names on,
    like mathematical equations,
    trying to figure out why you plus me
    never made one
I'm even afraid of sleeping
You see I keep dreaming of you and I
    making love like art in motion,
    frolicking in the fifth dimension
    like those days I laid inside you
    listening to Amos Lee songs;
    the days in your arms I felt God's salvation
    when I laid beside you completely void of motion;
    cold tears seeping into your skin
    as I unbottled emotions
And I'm afraid to speak of the tear-soaked spot
    on my bedroom floor where my knees sat
    seeking God in the faithless words I spoke
    that broke free from my broken soul
I'm afraid to tell the them that I was afraid
    when you told me,
    "This is where our story ends"

When those words left your fingers' tips,
    erasing from eternity the journey
    I wanted to die walking,
    my heart transitioned from being cracked
    to being completely broken

Bare

I've since spent days questioning that night,
    smiling at the picture before the fight,
    wiping tears that blurred my eyes on that
    dreadfully long ride to lonesomeness,
    the incarnation of my madness
I remember trying to close my eyes to lock inside
    the tears you weren't worth crying,
    but my lips sipped of the grief
My heart was burning,
    and I know you saw the smoking rising,
    signaling you that the one who loved you most
    was dying,
    but you craved sweet lies from strange lips
    though my kisses told you every single time,
    to me you were perfect
But I promise...
One day I'll finally walk away
But till then I'll just stand here,
    a victim of the apocalypse in my chaotic head
    watching you dreaming naked in my bed,
    but you see... I am alone
Confined inside myself
Hiding in shadows like cave dwelling creatures
    because your darkness showed me
    beautiful things about myself
So I'll be leaving
But God, I really miss not trying to defy your gravity,
    orbiting your entirety,
    perpetually falling,
    inevitably dying
You see you were my sun, Darling
My moon even
The constellation of complication
    that gave me direction
    each morning I rose like a man
    of no possessions
    on his road to perdition

C. L. Brown

Now I'm lying in your absence,
    pretending my lips
    are pressed up against your skin,
    pointing,
    tracing your contour,
    seeking,
    hoping
Praying someday you'll let me back in
Because like Adam having all his bones,
    I am so alone
Sometimes I think I'm going crazy,
    because I keep writing dark poetry
    imagining you're lying next to me,
    cold and alone in my house of stone
Because you see Darling,
    you were my home

But last night I wrote myself a letter
Told myself I'd be better
I'd be wiser
I'd be stronger
I'd find a better lover
But I was lying
See Darling, I'm dying
But I'm still fighting
Because my mind keeps bleeding,
So I keep writing,
    hiding inside the words you loved reading;
    still telling you the prettiest things
And I'm still waiting, for you

To drink you like fairytale poison,
    I mean potion,
    because I,
    like a lonely river,
    am running,
    but you,

Bare

    my ocean,
    are missing
You see my heart, my head, they're expanding
My chest, my lungs they're collapsing
My nose, my nostrils aren't breathing
Darling! I'm suffocating!
Hands clasping pretending I'm praying,
    but these telling tears...
    they won't stop running

And did I tell you that I miss you... Darling?
I think so
Some twenty something lines ago
But let's move on with this piece
    while I still have a piece
    of the peace you took
    when you said, "Peace!"

You see I was happy...
With you
And I was sad...
With you
Some days I was angry...
At you
But God, I really, really loved lying in sin...
With you

I miss having you for breakfast,
    dining in the kitchen
Breaking my fast from your skin
    craving the cauldron of ecstasy I always felt
    when wide open you took me in,
    and you became like sugar crystals
    melting in the fire rising from our sin
And when I have these thoughts
    it makes it hard breathing
You see I keep thinking,

C. L. Brown

    someday...
    maybe...
    one day...
You'll say, "I am still your everything, Darling"
And we'll rise again
    like morning suns leaving oceans
And we'll remember where we fell in love,
    and just the way it happened
And we'll touch each other again
    like mysterious objects of affection
    gifted from Heaven
And you, God's magnum opus,
    I will sing,
    playing familiar strings inside your darkness,
    once more seeing my broken pieces mending,
    becoming the man I was to be,
    for you

Bare

Freedom

I see you, my Darling
I see you, my true and deepest desire
How long I have waited to find
    my place in your arms
My time has finally come,
    and I am feeling so alone
Here I am alone in this dreadful cold,
    and your love can't stay his hands
Do you not see?
Death has come to stake its claim
My blood runs cold in all my veins
My feet are so tired of running
My hands are weary of praying
I can feel burdens lifting
Listen!
Listen to the slowing beat of my valiant heart
I am dying my Sweetheart
Because I'm unable to sustain when we are apart
I take air into my lungs prolonging
    my desperate plea that you'll hold me
    before I fall off my knees
But it appears my voice is fading
    because you aren't reacting
    to the pleas that are rising from my depths
So I am giving up this fight
Because I had a dream as I laid resting in the night
The moon gave not her light
The stars were nowhere in sight
The gelid wind pierced every inch of
    my pitted skin
I was so afraid
Lost in the womb of the cold and bitter night
How desperately I needed your light
Because I couldn't see the breaking
    of the new day

C. L. Brown

The terror took my voice
    as I screamed in the lightless night
    begging you, "please stay"
O the mockery of the darkness
I was engulfed in total madness
Deafened by the loudest of silence
Because your voice was no longer home

I closed my eyes fighting my best fight,
    but couldn't remember the taste of your lips
I couldn't remember the softness of your touch
    against my nakedness
    when your heart held pretty secrets
    it wanted to speak
I grew so dark outside of you
So I pray to God in the next cycle
    I'll have just one sip, of you
Because I will never grow sick, of you
So I made ready my body for the
    closing ceremony
But then my heart remembered
My heart remembered you, my Darling
And as the still ocean
    lying beneath the sleeping wind
My soul felt comforted
My soul felt liberated
Because you revived my dying heart
    rippling through fading memories

But to what purpose was I given life?
To live without you?
To live outside of your eyes?
This, my Sweetheart, isn't life
These nights my soul has poured out
    through my eyes secrets I held sacredly of you
With you
For you

Bare

For the day I was to wrap my arms around you
To tell you
How very much I love you
How very much I need you
But you've left me
And now I see...
I see your flower taking by the restless wind
Rising!
Rising!
I see the Light's arms reaching to embrace
    my beautiful grace
And now I am leaving this place
So I'll see you, my Darling
My sweetest Darling
My salvation
My eternal inspiration
See now
Death has come now
I am his now
So please, let me go

C. L. Brown

> My search for God was fruitless, until she opened her eyes.

Bare

Naked Poem

And then my soul saw her
    and it kind of went,
    "Oh, there you are.
    I've been looking for you"
And she said, "Me? But why?"
And I said,
    because I see the prettiest version of myself
    when I'm inside your eyes
And she smiled when for the first time
    she saw how God sees her,
    because my eyes could no longer keep His secret
Blushingly she bit her bottom lip
Then the sun,
    sneaking through diversely colored leaves,
    snuck a kiss upon her lips
And it made me jealous
And the wind flirted with her hair
    whispering sweetly into her ear
And it made me envious
And the Nightingale sang stealing her attention
And it made me nervous
But then she walked over
Her bare feet cradled in the soul of the earth
    lying between us
Then gently she traced her fingers
    down my cheek then across my lips
In silence I closed my eyes beneath
    the spell of love she casted over me
She asked, "What are you thinking?"
I said, Nothing!
But her keen eyes read the truth in this white lie
    I had written against my darkened soul
"Tell me", she pressed me
And so I confessed,
    it's just that each time you touch my skin

C. L. Brown

    my soul captures your fingers' prints
I said,
    I'm only so much familiar with God,
    but I'm quite certain He's grown tired of me now
She asked, "Why?"
And I said,
    because each time the ocean
    gives birth to the moon,
    I pray for you
And each time the clouds have need to shed burdens,
    I ask Him to shelter you
And each time the sun reminds me
    to open my eyes,
    I remind Him just how very much I love you
So you see, I can't help always thinking about you
Then she asked,
    "How come you always speak so poetically?"
And I said,
    because you always inspire me
She asked, "What do you mean?"
So I said,
    the way you utilize patience with my timid lips,
    the careful manner in which your eyes search me,
    the elegance in your fingers passing over my skin,
    the love reassuring me in your arms
    when I find myself inside them,
    the alluring protrusion of your hips,
    the lines that form next to your eyes
    each time you smile,
    the way your bare skin feels next to mine,
    the curls in your hair,
    the curious look in your eyes
    when your heart has questions,
    the sweet familiar feeling I get
    when your face falls between my chest
    and my chin, and your hands on
    the back of my neck feels as though

Bare

I'm being kissed by the gentlest wind,
your soul,
the conspiracy between your eyes
and your lips to steal my heart
each time I see you,
the way you speak of love,
the beauty of your thoughts,
the way you are able to instill peace
inside my soul when my mind
becomes like the angriest of stormy seas...
I said it's crazy, but even the way you call me "Baby",
   it's all poetry to me
Then she hugged me, and I felt warm tears
   against the right side of my face
So I said,
   are you hurting, Darling?
And she said,
   "I just really really love who I am
     when I'm inside of you"
So I snuggled her heart in the purest of love,
   and tucked it extremely deep inside my own
The I said,
   I'm so delighted to know that
   of all the places in this entire Creation,
   it is inside of you that I feel most at home
It is only inside of you that I am never alone

And that is why when my soul saw her
   it kind of went,
     "Oh, there you are.
     I've been looking for you."
And if she still doesn't understand why,
   or she just feels like pretending,
   I will gladly spend the next thousand
   lifetimes with her face tucked between
   my chest and my chin
   as I read for her, this naked poem

C. L. Brown

> Never underestimate the power within a smile given to repel the darkness bearing your brokenness.

Bare

Residue

A ghost lingers within my shadows
And fear triumphs courage,
    as I sink deeper in this heart-wrenching love
    I can't let go
I am haunted by your smile
    when I desire love's fading
    like black smoke in the restless wind
I seek comfort with spirits,
    emptying bottles,
    spilling secrets,
    but that is where you reside most
Every sip is a dose of some memory;
    those better days you spent
    in quietude next me
Taking my rational self away from myself,
    and I am here with you again
    as you materialize in my emotions,
    and I question my sanity
    in light of my heart's delight
Trying to drink away these fears
    wiping warm tears because you aren't here
The silence amplifies your voice inside my head
My arms, and my lips often pretend
    you still have a place in my bed
So I hold your ghost,
    pressing my fingers into your skin
Watching your love fade
    because I'm helpless where
    my heart is concerned
He begs me to reach out for his life,
    but this pride...
My passion is that fire the rain hates to fight,
    still burning,
    still praying...
    one of these days, my Darling...

C. L. Brown

This residue in my head will be a wildfire
    in my arms as you were in the good days
Then I will lose sight of the visions of his lips
    searching out the things I hid inside of you
They at times compel me not to breathe,
    placing me in the balance,
        where salvation judges between my afflicted heart,
        and a chick's feather

Barc

Embrace of Death

Her conflagration engulfed me
    as a moisture-less twig,
    and I capitulated,
    allowing her to purge my fallible existence
And there,
    while blazing,
    smoke rising from my skin
    as her flaming fingers absolved my accursed soul
I gave thanks to my King for being so forgiving
Watching her whipping me into submission,
    taking lashes at my flesh like the cat o' nine

In her arms I was taken to the brink of death
    where I lost the fight losing my breath
So finally, having experienced the very best thing
    this side of Heaven
I gave up the ghost,
    but her soul and mine had unfinished business
Tell me, have you witnessed the beauty
    of naked souls making poetry outside of carnality?
Ah, how sweet the embrace of death

C. L. Brown

Specter

Perfect art is her naked soul
Just the way I perceive her
    in thoughts I have not spoken
On rainy days, she dances with freedom
She's God's voice calling,
    and I am dying to see her smile in life's parallel
But she's so lovely when her calming voice fills me
Her perfectly naked soul is perfect artistry
Her alluring radiance and freckled nose
Making me feel things completely foreign

Naked in my arms,
    I AM her sun finding reasons
    to rise, and fall against her skin
Allowing her to bloom in a love
    that is never out of season

On rainy days, she dances with freedom
But spirits in my head
    kept her bound in my bed,
    and now I've written them
In love I birthed them
Kissing her ghost
Reading her skin
Wishing on dying stars
    because I yearn to replenish the earth
    with multiple versions of this flawless
    likeness of God
I hunger for a taste of the things
    she has yet spoken;
    to read emotions in her eyes while
    every inch of my covering interprets them
Her apparition is my prison
Her lips are the hands of God
    shaping my soul as she sees fit

Barc

On rainy days, she dances with freedom
She is the colors of the dreams keeping my eyes open,
    though darkness fights them

My silence gives her wings
A place inside my sacred heart to play her strings
Sacrificing her divine,
    she's falling,
    because I'm forsaken
My purpose was conceived in her voice speaking life
    into my void
And she has known love
For she has felt me
On rainy days, she dances with freedom
In my morning she's the departed sun rising,
    driving the cold fingers of fear from my skin
She's a song departing the sacred lips
    God spoke with in the genesis of Creation
And on rainy days, she dances with freedom

C. L. Brown

Crossing
(For Keisha... Remembering Jason)

I wish to God it was loose imaginations
Flipping through pictures like Holy Scriptures
Trying to find peace of mind in this sea of anger,
    because I heard from a stranger,
    you're no longer breathing

Now should I rip this heart from my chest,
    and showed it to you beating in my hand
    pleading for life as my spirit makes
    its grand escape,
    would you believe that I am broken?
If I took you into my mind,
    and showed you the immeasurable reasons
    why I cannot find the sleep
    my eyes keep seeking,
    fighting but can't keep at bay these demons,
    would you even care?
If I lose myself before God,
    pouring pain from within
    like watering eyes with unbearable grief,
    tears running like rivers
    saturating mascara-soiled sheets,
    would He hear me?
Would He even think to console me?
Lord knows I keep praying,
    but it seems before they even leave my mouth,
    the words fall to the floor,
    watered down in the pool of tears
    settling at my feet

He said He's closer than a friend
But does He understand
    that right now,
    in this very moment

Bare

   I
    feel
        like
            I
              am
                  dying?

Against the naked backdrop
   of white and gray clouds
   concealing the pretty blue,
   I see your spirit rising
Leaving me here to relive our best days
   through outdated conversations now fading
You see there is a battlefield in my mind,
   and I am fighting so hard,
   but it seem I'm losing

Apply pressure to the wound
   the voice keeps crying,
   but the pain just keeps pouring out,
   and these repressed words are stuck in my throat;
   evident in the silence of my screams

But you don't understand
Do you?
Can you see the frown in my smile?
Cause I swear my face puts no face to the faces
   my heart is making behind the veil
   that now stands between me and you

It's raining inside here
Though the sun is never more watchful
How fitting, right?
The world goes to sleep,
   but I just sit staring off into the night
And where is the Son when you need Him?
He said if you're in need just call Him

C. L. Brown

But I've lost my voice from this persistent crying,
    screaming,
        thinking somehow the hurt will
        leave me forsaken come next morning
Teetering between laughter and pain
Because through their questions
    I relive it all again
Holding myself because I feel no one understands
Plus I can't find my peace
    in the embrace of strange hands
So I'm searching these tears for answers
Hoping these waters will make me anew...
    cause Jesus wept

Thoughts like butterflies' wings
    caught in turbulent winds
    rocking me, but my mind won't sleep
    and no matter how good the food
    you brought smells, I just can't eat
Face wedged between my knees
    staring this last hour at me feet,
    because I want to leave this place of pain,
    but like my soul,
    they are so tired
Time is so merciless
Opening windows to brick walls
    when the wings I can't grow desire open skies
But this chain at my feet
Rusting against my skin
Clanging with each step taken
    in this tiny cell of pain-painted walls,
    and bars of hope thinking it's all a joke
    as I reach for a hand, but felt no one
My mind sat on that rope hanging above my head
    calling my name;
    promising freedom from this house of pain,
    but I am conflicted

Bare

So please turn off this silence
Turn off this mind in my head
    that won't keep quiet
    even when I lay seeking death in my own bed
Turn of the cliché-saturated speeches
    breaking their lips telling me
    everything will be OK

Turn it all off!

My knees have become my favored position
Asking God please help me make it
    over this mountain
I know you've done it many times before
    and they say have faith,
    but my mind is busy,
    my eyes are watery,
    my feet can't carry me,
    my hands can't comfort me,
    my words have forsaken me,
    and no matter how hard I look
    at my reflection, all I see is a broken
    image reflecting my pieces falling
    to the pile mounting at my feet

So I ask you...
If I ripped my blood-soaked heart from my chest
    and showed it to you,
    beating in my hand,
    begging for life as his spirit
    makes its grand escape,
    would you believe,
    that I am broken?

C. L. Brown

Colorful Resentment

I'm having a hard time getting past
    the profane words we spoke
        breaking beautiful souls to appease brutish egos
Last night and the other night
    plus the other night we were right
Everything was tight
Arms around shoulders squeezing waistlines,
    slow dancing drinking aged wine,
        getting lost in the conversations we held
        beneath perfect silence
Not a reason under the heavens
    to drive a wedge between us
But now...
I'm sifting cluttered memories
Slow sipping expensive liquor
    trying to intoxicate every part of my being
    that misses the sweet taste
    of your poisonous tongue

You're like that song I love to hate
The one they played on our first date
    that reminds me how much I still love you
My mind keeps you on repeat
My battered heart keeps skipping vital beats,
    because of the heat of the words you spoke
    that kept me from sleep
But let me burn
Perhaps then the shit you took
    will find itself in my next book
    like the picture I took of you and him
Hands locked
Fingers entwined
Him touching your skin, getting me aroused
But I'll scratch this broken record
    and play the next track

Bare

    as I lay flat thinking of your legs
    wrapped around my back

You used to be mine
So divinely fine
And now...
I'm sitting here writing bitter ass poetry
    hoping between these lines
    you'll see all that you meant to me;
Hoping you'll find reasons again to fall for the man
    who still yearns to love you;
    albeit with a broken heart

C. L. Brown

> A miracle birthed outside its season is a complication. Be patient.

Bare

Soliloquy

I found you adrift inside my serenity
This path traveled least
Your feet submerged deep inside of me,
    because I crave the affection I only receive
    lying between sex-scented sheets
    as you feast upon my nakedness
My soul has never been more famished,
    but when you begged,
    I opened myself receiving your darkness;
    now your seed inside me grows,
    rooted so deep inside my soul
    I'll have to excavate my Truth
    just to get rid of you
My trust you've sown inside carefully
    cultivated lies; now I bear fruit
    each time we lie polluting my truth
    as you contaminate my soul,
    syphoning life between my thighs
So think what you will,
    but I AM the manifestation of thoughts
    God hasn't spoken, evoking your inception
    long before your wretched soul
    ever needed salvation
I AM your breath of life drawn from
    the sacred black hole of God's soul
I AM more than the silk-like sun-kissed skin
    inciting lust-filled words
    from that pitch black heart
    that lacks understanding

I was there at the beginning
Long before time took form
Before galaxies were born
When God said let's make her like Him
Then I opened my womb

C. L. Brown

    giving birth to the balance of
    love and compassion,
    He called you Adam
Before the dawn of the sun's initial rising,
    I was the deep darkness the Spirit summoned,
    awakening my soul from precious sleep
It was then that I opened myself
    birthing flesh and bones,
    shaping love like wet clay in gifted hands;
    allowing the man to taste the sacred truths
    of His unspoken thoughts

But I remain a mystery,
    because you refuse to see that
    each time you attempt to break me,
    you pile fertilized soil over divine purpose
And it appears you didn't know this,
    but the best thing you could ever do to a
    seed,
    is bury it

I AM the melanin lining your skin,
    connecting your unlit soul to the
    Light-bearing Son,
    syphoning life from His Light,
    though you stand before Him dying
I AM the sustenance sent of Him
    to supply your soul,
    and I am here,
    but there you remain craving flesh
    with your tongue hanging like dogs panting,
    because you are yet blind in the Light
    of the purpose in my breast

I am that Lotus
Your sacred flower
Rooted in infidelity, pain, sadness, and anger

Bare

Seeded in the lies you tell yourself
    in that futile effort to persuade yourself
    that I am not worthy to be held
    in the pure bliss of love's embrace
But when your lustful soul sought its next victim,
    it was me,
    the trail of dirt,
    that you were caught sinking those fingers in

For once I wish you would close those eyes
    that you may see that though I draw life from
    your murky waters,
    I AM still that sacred flower;
    untouched by the words you spoke
    that should have died in your throat,
    unscathed by the thoughts you wrote
    slicing my skin;
    for though I appeared weakened,
    I bled beauty, grace, elegance,
    and perfection

But the truth is,
    I AM the dirt that you think of me
The soil your withering soul is rooted in
And so you walk over the soul
    of the path least traveled,
    plucking my petals,
    prematurely exposing my virgin flower

And just imagine,
    nine months in my womb I carried you,
    loving you,
    protecting you,
    but it appears you've forgotten
    our beautiful connection
So here, let me help your recollection
See inside my soul your divine reflection

C. L. Brown

    reflected in the essence of
    your wife,
    your sister,
    your mother,
    and your precious daughter
Because I see you in your slumber,
    referring to me as another
See first I was your "Trick"
    though I tried freeing you from this darkness
Now I'm the "Bad Bitch" on every track
    as you leave tracks in my soul
    like community needle's holes;
    losing sight of the fact that before you had
    the God-given blessing to sing,
    I held you covered in the birth fluid
    still dripping from your wrinkled skin,
    as I sat there hemorrhaging between my legs;
    when you sucked from my breast life,
    because I loved you more than myself

So now I give birth to the legacy
    He's seeded me
Sowing these words
    emancipating the masculine facet
    of our divine balance;
    leaving unspiritual babe-minded men
    asking questions

And so it is,
    I AM the dirt that you think of me
But I AM beautiful, powerful, and divine
I AM God's fingers
    passing over your broken skin
    healing every bruise, crack, scratch,
    and swelling
I AM the moon
    cradling you inside my womb

Bare

    each night your darkness falls
I AM your heart's beat
I AM your place of rest
    after you've been beaten down in those streets
I AM your love
I AM your strength
I AM your grace

I AM your wife,
I AM your sister,
I AM your mother,
    and your precious daughter
I, AM Eve

C. L. Brown

Songbird
(Remembering Dr. Maya Angelou)

For I am
    the Songbird who sang
        Phenomenal Woman
The fathomless soul
    deeper than oceans' secrets
How tenderly I've incubated them when strength
    departed eager souls as aged leaves
        having fulfilled their purpose
My song is yet written in the wind
Odes of gallantry sung by timeless souls
    are now your heritage
So sing my darlings
Just sing

Bare

The palms of Love are always faced down.

C. L. Brown

Praying Hands

I have seen the deaths of suns
I have seen hope falling like frail leaves
    in the wake of Autumn's breeze
I have seen the births of moons;
    that subtle reminder that tomorrow comes
    to mend yesterday's wounds
I have fought to snatch my life
    from the cold hands of time,
    losing pieces of the most precious piece
    God's ever laid fingers on
And I...
I have heard the words they spoke
    summoning death from conniving lips;
    hoping I'd never find a place on my knees,
    that place God, and men eventually meet
I have felt the anguish
    of words marring my heart's canvas,
    defacing the masterpiece love gifted;
    watching sacred love streaming to my feet,
    wasted
I have felt the seclusion of lonesome rooms
    when the frigid grip of fear compelled me
    to shed burdensome secrets with pillows,
    and black sheets
I
Am
Searching
But can't find any relief
Is it the peaceful rest of the mockingbird,
    her wings having exhausted the wind,
    or the conquest of the grave's darkness?
Are the songs sung in memory of what was,
    or the praise of what shall be?
It's all the same to me now
Now that the end has finally come

Bare

I long to see the clasping
    of Mama's praying hands
I miss the songs birthed in the deep of her silence
    that penetrated my juvenile bones,
    quieting fears I was to fashion from ignorance
There was healing in her lips,
    and I remember her words
    mending my broken spirit
But I am the seed sown in arid dirt,
    mastering mettle,
    and to God be the glory
Some days my mind goes ahead of myself,
    and I am with love again,
    and she feels as perfect as she did back then
I know death inches his way
    through the clefts of my soul,
    but am I that man walking these streets,
    chains clanging at my feet,
    thinking I be free?

All my days I've been a slave to the sway
    in untamed trees
All my days I've seen their leaves making merry
    in the tender breeze
All my days I've seen life submitting to death
All my days I've seen courage gasping
    for that last breath
But in all my days,
    and in all the stupendous wonders I've seen,
    Mama's praying hands are still
    the most beautiful thing in that distant memory

C. L. Brown

> When the seed enters the soil does it pray for a miracle, or does it take advantage of what has already been provided?

Bare

Wine Tasting

Our souls submitted to flesh
Perpetuity risking death,
    experiencing breaths of mind bending passion
Countless times in that split second
    I tasted Heaven through the perfect slit
    unhurried hands crafted into her divine,
    grafting myself into the source of her beautiful
My words patiently stripped away the lies
    she clothed herself in distracting those who
    lacked the wisdom needed to see that
    time eventually reveals her Truth
Then I laid her, gently, naked in my head
Vintage red wine taking her mind to slow and easy
Her leisurely fingers searching that supernal body
My tongue feeling envious,
    falling in love with the way she teased me
I raised my attention allowing her to take sips
    of the eternal me,
    perpetuating the fire lit to consume her forever
She permitted my teeth to take part
    in the masterpiece my lips were painting,
    and I dipped my tongue into her water colors,
    leaving bristle tracks all over her canvas
Then I poured aged grapes on her flesh,
    licking every single runaway stream
    from her toes to her neck
Eyes closed she witnessed the manifestation
    of secrets I held scheming to rewrite
    the climax of her eternity
And she feasted on my lines as cured spirits
    syphoned honesty out of my lies
Conversing with her mind, I whispered things
    that made her feel as though she was being eaten
    with calculated patience

C. L. Brown

Songstress

This is for the Songstress,
    masking the broken soul,
    melding broken poetry
    with her broken melody
How gracefully she discarded my fears
    with poetic expressions until my petrified
    mind found its freedom there within herself
It seems only yesterday,
    because I can still see myself sifting the smog
    in that sweaty 2nd floor curbside café
Getting caught in her gravity,
    falling without a fight into the blue words
    ascending from her darkness
You should see it,
    how beautifully she stripped me bare
    of inhibited aspirations

I remember polluting my virgin lungs
    with illegal Cubans;
        peering through the sheer curtain-like smoke
        rising from my indecent lips
I still remember tasting her soft brown
    complexion; ingesting her skin-tone
    as I slow sipped her desire
    between shots of Tennessee Fire
I remember trying to still
    the tremor in my hand that made it hard
    holding the half empty glass steadily
    against my lust-filled lips
Completely nervous, because everything
    about her brokenness was perfect

The medley of emotions finding freedom,
    revealing her longing to be held
    in arms that understood patience

Bare

The cold tears cascading from her cold eyes
    infused with the black mascara
    she tried hiding white lies behind
The see-through dress
    with the high rising slit
    exposing things private my lips coveted
The maturation of seductive lyrics
    seeping through those saccharine lips,
    accentuating her sexy

I remember her repeated cries for the Lord
    as one weighted down by tremendous burdens;
    losing herself in the conversation we held
    between the melancholic riffs escaping
    plucked instruments
I remember reflecting on her reflection
    taking that bottle to my lips
    as I swallowed deep secrets,
    internalizing her story,
    being possessed by the sweet spirits trapped
    inside her Tennessee Honey

I was emptying bottles getting woozy
She was emptying secrets
    spitting provocative truths
    in the microphone's chrome-plated tip,
    arresting my attention the way she
    wrapped those inquisitive fingers around it
I remember how she moved
    like the smooth soul of Caribbean palm trees
    dancing in the ocean-whispered gentle breeze
Swaying those hips,
    synchronizing her soul with the
    resonating bassline's hits
I remember how she stroked my intentions
    erecting fading emotions,
    allowing me to relive her again and again

C. L. Brown

I remember rising and then falling,
    living and then dying with her pulse
    as I pulsated beneath my shame
    with every note that she sung,
    whispering my name

And as though she wasn't already mine,
    I took time pillaging her passions,
    finding my whole new world
    just beyond her mysterious ocean
It was then I became lost in her eyes,
    and she saw it
It was then she began mounting my rise,
    I could feel it
The way her eyes pierced the thick
    smoke rising from the hell-like flame
    that raged deep inside my sinful soul
Lord have mercy!
I wanted so badly to spend time like those
    with criminal minds,
    feasting completely on her naked body
Slow sipping that fine Tennessee Whiskey,
    growing more and more inebriated,
    losing inhibitions in her beguiling eyes

So as the sun fell between the astral planes
    of her multifaceted dimensions,
    we patiently shared space outside of time
    as I made divine love to her secular soul
My tongue showed pardon administering her healing,
    confessing unforgiven sins
    as I submitted myself beneath her purified Truth
    while she melted in my mouth
    like whiskey-infused ice cubes

It was seven times in seven nights in the nucleus
    of her earthbound Heaven,

Bare

    that I pervaded her soul again and again
    slow sipping Old No. 7
My eyes witnessing my thoughts
    dictating to my hands
    as they repeatedly took her to my lips
    until she was completely empty
I was caressing her gently,
    promising sincerely I'd conceal her secrets
Hence she confided in the lips that were destined
    to expose the sweetness overflowing
    the treasure trove buried beneath her rainbow
So I stand now a victim of the spell casted
    in light of my betrayal
A slave to the memory of that beautiful Songstress
    as she abused the microphone's chrome-plated
    tip, arresting my attention,
    with that old Tennessee Blues type of music

C. L. Brown

Waiting

Catch me
I'm falling
Hold me
I'm dying
Feel my tears against your skin
They convey messages I've been writing
    since that very first morning
Tell me everything
So in the crossing
I will forget not even the simplest thing
Speak to me the way you used to
Call me Darling
Because the sun fades
The Sky folds
But I remember the first place
When for the first time your lips parted,
    and your divine self whispered to mine
I remember the color of the sun's reflection
    in your curious eyes
I remember the perfect crookedness
    of your unmatched smile
I remember it all
But my mind is slowing
My speech is slurring
My heart's beat is fading
But I'm trying to hold on to what gave me reason
    to love the most beautiful love
        God had anything to do with
Here after
When my flesh sprouts roots in the earth,
    and my spirit moves like spring's leaves
        in that slow dance with the benevolent breeze
What will I become?
Will my path be as lit as the sun?
Or Will darkness scream, "Welcome!"?

Bare

What if I be alone?
Will you be OK with me wanting to come home?
Will you love me still should I not return?
What will I become?
What will fear make of me
    knowing where I go you cannot come?
I don't know how to be
If you are not with me
I don't know where to go without my direction
    etched inside of you
They say love leads destined souls back home
But my fingers are now cold
And these thoughts in my heart
    I wish to speak before I depart,
    but my lips are too weak to split apart
So I trust that you know my heart
I trust you heard it all
Every single whisper of love through these
    tributaries of tears seeping into your skin
Because as much as I want to refrain
    from answering His calling
Death is waiting
And I can't stop my eyes' closing
But I will be waiting for that next time
When for the first time,
    your essence will be one with mine

C. L. Brown

> If God truly is Love then the single greatest thing you could ever do is to love someone purely. There is no higher level of consciousness. For love is not the essence of a word spoken. Love is the essence of the one who expresses God in the totality of their being. That is immortality, and there is nothing greater.

Bare

Procession to Freedom

Take me into the deep
Where sweet songs pacify my troubled heart
Sing for me in the deep
Bury my cares in the sea of love

Take me into the deep
Where sweet songs pacify my troubled mind
Listen to their voices,
    sing o children,
    stir those waves of virtue
Here in the deep,
    where my soul's rusted chains shall be broken

Walk with me into the deep
Where aged cares fall to unshackled feet
Bury me in the deep
Bury my sins in the ocean's soul

O God, here me now
My shout is no longer silenced
For death has passed by my sacred abode
So will you not hear me now, o God?

O death
O silence
O sin
Release me now
For long have I waited on the Son
Long have I waited,
    and now the moon has hidden her face
So o God, hear me now
Bury my sins in the ocean's soul
Where sweet songs pacify my troubled heart

C. L. Brown

Falling

I love you, simply
I need you, desperately
To be fused with every single cell
    in your flawless body

I think of you
    on days when the world invades my head
I break away from it all,
    watching you through silence,
    exhaling pieces of dreams I'm dying
    to share with you
Inhaling pieces of myself I've kept
    safe all my days, just for you

I'm falling,
    dying to everything that stood contrary
    to this love burning inside the heart you left

Bare

Cosmic Dance

I sense your sadness orbiting your pain
Watching you sitting there again
Memories exhausting your worrisome mind,
    and I can't help wishing you were mine
I hopelessly wish to be the only reason
    your heart decides some things
    are still worth loving
I covet to guard your dearest secret
    whenever your heart feels comfort in my eyes,
    finding reasons to reveal it
I want so badly to study your chemistry
Amalgamating pieces of you with pieces of me
Cause I need you to know that
    you're the only one for me
To tap into your cosmic energy
Stealing loose electrons
    to balance these naked protons,
    fortifying my photons of consciousness,
    because imbalance is contrary to divine destiny
And I can see clearly,
    you're already the very best of me
I wish desperately to set free unspoken intentions
Invading your existence
Pervading your cosmic core
Piercing your elusive black hole
Colliding with your soul
Creating worlds our future selves will inhabit
I wish eagerly to make you my habit
Just give me 21 days
24 hours each;
    to repeat you between white cotton sheets
    as I dive deep into the mysteries of the art
    time kept from your broken past

C. L. Brown

> Forgiveness is a gift to both the forgiver, and the one being forgiven. It is a clean slate. A chance, not necessarily to continue, but to start anew. Quite certainly however, it is not meant to be used as a roadmap back to pain.

Bare

Waste

Regrettably your words still remain
Those permanent black stains
    desecrating the snow-white essence
    I loved you from
Most nights it seems the stars hide,
    and I find myself wiping cold tears
    streaming from bloodshot eyes,
    because you've blurred all signs leading to the
    beautiful future our dark past promised me
You took the love that balanced me,
    and I read your lies in my eyes
    every single time I stare in the mirror
Your name is a persistent reminder
    of the agonizing pain you inflicted
    with each step I stumbled with
    trying to find myself again
Walking backwards motion slowed in my feet
    trying to find where it was we found solace
    in the wrong direction
Watching myself trapped inside the allegory
    written beneath your beautiful
Shadows depicting broken feelings
    in the soiled thoughts where
    I sowed your damaged seed,
    hoping to set you free you from yourself
Hoping you'd bear fruit inside of me,
    but now I'm afraid to give again the pieces
    of myself that replaced the missing pieces
    of your porous heart

I'm still trying to understand the empty meaning
    of your sinful lips against my skin
Still trying to understand why I keep wasting
    precious time between them as though it is
    your name that shall bring my salvation

C. L. Brown

Still trying to understand why it is I stand damned
    having committed no sin
    while you wash those filthy hands
    pretending you had no part
    in what I've become

My thoughts were as pure as mountain-cap snow,
    and that is where I kept you
Where the common pitfalls of blooming hearts
    couldn't reach you
I watched my words picking at your soul
    removing those things that kept you
    from the best version of yourself
Defying the counsel of the council in my head,
    I've slept with your ghost in my undefiled bed,
    because my foolish heart was too foolish
    to see the fool you made of me
But I'm still looking back
    trying to see past the fact
    that you never truly saw me,
    and that's fact because your hands
    never took the time to flip through the pages
    of the book I emptied myself in;
    telling tales of the freckle-faced girl
    with the caramel tight girls
    who captured everything about me

I was satisfied at your empty table,
    scripting sacred thoughts
    adding pages to the fable
Refusing to see past the reality
    that eventually we'd be just dust
But I was impaired of judgement,
    sipping fine wine from your empty glass
Finding consolation in words you never spoke
Painting the picture I pictured;
    now staring at this blank canvas

Bare

    trying to decipher the picture
    perpetuating the pleasures of the foolish heart
    that still refuses to see that the pages were
    written on with powdered sand,
    and now the silent wind has spoken,
    but I am here pretending I'm not broken
But "I see you",
    "I adore you",
        "I trust you",
            "I want, and need you"...
These words I bled though never explicitly said
    as the heart hemorrhaged slowly
    whispering goodbye,
    because you still wouldn't look me in the eye

I've spent my last emotion
    dwelling on the notion that you actually cared
Trapping thoughts on paper about it,
    then reading between the lines
    the lies you tried feeding me,
    because you knew I was hungry
But I'm still depending on this flame
    raging inside my chest,
    burning in my flesh,
    to set free myself inside your skin
I'm trying to control these emotions
    because every fiber of my being
    has been screaming your name
    since the second you left me
I've tried what you told me,
    crying in the rain,
    but your stains still remain;
    a constant reminder of the one I am foolishly
    trying to find again

C. L. Brown

It is foolish for one to water a plant they don't which to see grow. When we supply things with our energy we empower them. They will take root in our lives. So, if we desire love, then we should speak more about loving and being loved, and less about being used and being broken. If we wish to be successful at something, we ought not speak more about failures than we do triumphs. A great deal of what we'll experience in this life has everything to do with what resides in our minds, and flows off our tongues. So, speak life, and leave death to the dead.

Bare

Lunacy

What possessed him,
   watering this dead flower?
Does love make mad
   those who choose rather
   to see chaos in order?
What is madness?
Is it not the soul void of love?
Is it not the one guided by the written rules
   of the fools not acquainted
   with the scars of fearless hearts?
Surely, some mime their way
   when the eyes are without purpose
But certainly, not them, the mad ones
The ones whose eyes have become one with darkness
The ones who disregard the authority of death
For what is death without life,
   and what is life without love?
Can death find purpose outside his flower?
So, what possessed him,
   watering this dead flower?
Why it is the very essence of them,
   those mad ones

C. L. Brown

Sand in the Wind

And when the ocean gave birth to her sun,
    we had an affair between words
    before the world that not a
    single soul understood outside us
She said my embrace epitomized trust
    as her eyes scavenged her pieces
        God hid beyond my flesh
The insolence of this free-spirited gale,
    rising in my calm,
    stirring my emotions,
    then leaving me to pick up the pieces
    she knows I'll never mend

I was the tranquil breeze
    breaking free from the ocean's quietude
Her skin was a welcoming sanctum,
    making me anew
But as our darkness unveiled the silvery moon
    giving rest to the love that rose between us;
    I inhaled every word I ever spoke
    in the smoke rising from her burning heart
And in the eyes of realization,
    her breath against my skin
    was but powdered sand in the wake
    of the rested wind

Bare

> When I was living, I thought about riches. Now that I'm dying, I think about love. I only wish I'd lived for what I'm dying for.

C. L. Brown

Emptied

With the pitch-black night sky
    laid at my fingers' tips like virgin paper
My nude thoughts decorated your art
    like stars decorate the womb of the night;
    speaking as God in the genesis of Creation,
    reading our conclusion is this revelation
    as I tried breathing life into dying memories,
    planting seeds I know
    will never see the light of day

Yes! I'm thinking of you again
Lost in the past
    staring at the rear-view mirror vibrating
    as my heart pounds for you
Looping played-out songs in my futile effort
    to rekindle the flame I dowsed
    when my lips gave passage to the things
    my mind never meant to say
I am as vacant as this empty road
    leading me away from the fullness
    my prideful heart cherished
    from the "Hello" I met in your eyes,
    to the last empty kiss
    you adorned my cheek with
Maybe I do deserve this

Bare

Addiction

I have an addiction to her poison
Tricky thing is, the remedy is woven into her skin
I know!
I risk death!
See, I found my soul in her lips,
    and God in her eyes,
       but there was that devil in her hips
       that made sweet the taste of sin
So with every sip of her sweet nectar I am dying
But life requires this choice of me
Besides the resurrection is foretold
Plus I love to watch her layers
    exfoliating between my fingers

C. L. Brown

Devil

I have seen the face of Satan
My father told me to embrace my demon
Said in his darkness I'd find vision
So I spent many days in his eyes
    trying to make truth of his lies,
    and now he's moved on,
    but my decaying soul here lies

I have seen the face of Satan
But funny enough he doesn't look
    as I'd imagined
I stood there, comparing his complexion to my skin
Father said those two were the same thing
But I know now he had not the pleasure
    of making his acquaintance

See he'd never felt his silk-like skin
He'd never conversed with his soul
    spending time between his lips,
    being a victim of that seductive kiss

I've seen the face of Satan
And curiosity had me to reach out,
    to wipe the mirror
I needed to see much clearer
But I found my fingers searching my own soul,
    being intimate with this cold stranger

So yes! I have seen the face of Satan,
    but I lived not to talk about it
So you ask, who then wrote this?
Do you not yet understand?

Bare

Pieces

There they all were...
Her nervous skin, and my forbearing fingers
Her broken soul, and my words
Her naked hips, and my lips
Her darkest fears, and my embrace
Her warm tears, and my shoulder
Her perfect eyes, and my hiding place
Her beautiful smile, and my comfort
Her love, and my freedom's wings
Her flavor, and my inquisitive tongue

My confusion, and her wisdom
My loneliness, and her presence
My aching body, and her healing touch
My need of poetic inspiration,
    and her divine vibration
My indecision, and her patience

Just pieces of her, and chunks of me,
    trying to make sense
    of the perfect imperfection that we were
Finding our place outside their space
Where the stars became envious
    of her gleam against my darkened soul,
    and the moon lived vicariously through a love
    as pure as the oxygen leaving new born leaves
Without this woman I care not to breathe
Pounding my fists against my head
    trying to erase her from my thoughts,
    shedding pieces of my own soul instead
The futile acts of a man
    dying to love a woman seeking freedom

C. L. Brown

> Treat the day as you would soil. Give to it what you want from it. Make it bless you.

Bare

Finders Keepers

Pretty the blue of his ocean's soul
Snaring wildly running clouds,
    and the parts of his being
        their eyes cannot see
Visions of freedom locked inside finite spaces,
    and he slew his freedom,
        refusing to be away from you
Mercy is within your hands
The same ones he's dying in
Brown is the color of his skin
    capturing the essence of your eyes,
        though you refuse to let him back in
So speak him out of your soul
Let him die in the misunderstandings
    of strange hearts
For to you, he is without leaves
But they somehow manage to indulge in the fruits
    of his naked branches

C. L. Brown

Broken Chain

She came by reason of my lips,
    though I've spoken not a single word
Said she hadn't known freedom,
    but at my behest she emptied herself,
    and not a single drop knew the floor
I found a place on my knees
    after she'd released;
    where thoughts brewing in my spirit ascended
    like smoke in thanksgiving for the night that
    trapped a piece of my soul
    in the fabric of her time
She's now free
I'm now a slave to the last hour
    she spent conquering me

Bare

Wildfire

My friends say I'm too lost inside of you
I smile at their madness
How can they even begin to fathom
    how lost I am being outside of you?
I am in love with the very breath
    that passes through your lungs
    as it expands your chest
    in response to the lessons
    my tongue impresses upon your soul,
    each time I fix it between
    those delectable lips
I have not a single wish
    to spend even a split second
    in a place, or time where you cannot be mine

You see with love, there is no negotiating
She requires everything,
    and everyone wants something,
    but at her table so many come offering nothing,
    yet expect to walk away with everything
But not me
I will offer the flesh upon my bones
I will offer the nothingness that I AM
I will offer the rest of my days
    to roam unpaved pathways void of sanity,
    just to sit one split second in a place, or time
    where you will be completely mine
Because you were the wildfire my
    sheltered soul needed
And I love you because you burned away
    every bit of who I was until I fell in love
    with the stranger who gave me purpose
Even now the days take my thoughts back to you,
    and the nights are pure bliss
    when in surreal dreams I am here again with you

C. L. Brown

Still very much lost in the depths of you
Perfecting my learning of loving you

Bare

Last Supper

I fixed a place of raw poetry
    that fits precisely
    the contour of her sinuous body
Then I traced her sultry curves
    with erotic words
    until she manifested between my fingers
Like the egret, my hands patiently
    stirred dormant passions
    as I foraged her wetlands dispelling hunger
I licked her pink hibiscus-like pigment
    as she bloomed in the relentless pursuits
    of a tongue endeavored to please
In the end,
    she took to her knees,
    shaking like young leaves
    arrested in turbulent breeze
Then I prayed as one satisfied
    at the conclusion of his last supper
Asking Him to bless
    the mouthwatering provisions I had indulged in;
    covering sins I had already committed

C. L. Brown

> If your search for God takes you to a place where hatred for others not like yourself has taken residence in your heart, know that either God was never there, or He has since moved on.

Bare

Redemption

If I die now, and I go to Heaven
Will I see Jesus?
Relieved of all my problems?

If Heaven doesn't want me,
    and I come back to you,
    would you hold like Jesus would?

If I find rest in the darkness,
    and it ceased the resounding sound in my chest,
    would my sins be purged?

If I break the flesh upon my knees,
    confessing unspoken nefarious deeds,
    will my soul be freed?

If I die now, and I go to Heaven
Will I see Jesus?
Be freed from all my problems?

If Heaven doesn't want me,
    and I come back to you,
    would you hold me like Jesus never could?

C. L. Brown

> You have to decide whether or not she's amazing. If she's not, set her free to be found by the one who's tirelessly searching for her. If she is, never let the sun trade places with the moon without letting her know that she is.

Bare

Denouement

He battered her petals in the tempest
    of the merciless words his
    fearful heart could not restrain
Such fragile a flower
That morning she found a way out of the
    broken pieces that had fallen against her feet,
    but following the trail of pain
    dripping from what she became,
    he wrapped those deceitful words
    around her soul again
But he was the mistake she resented herself
    for making
The same one she couldn't help repeating
At each meeting he held her as it were his
    life God hid inside her flesh,
    and death was famished
But he couldn't speak peace over the storm
    surging in her eyes
Countless the nights,
    submitting to the
    fear she felt inside,
    her heart questioned him,
    "Do you still love me, Darling?"
But lies the color of moonless nights concealed
    the secrets he poisoned her soul with
In solitude she screamed in silence
Dry-eyed she cried
    as his lies slowly pierced the last bit
    of hope that kept her afloat
    off the lust-stained floor beneath his nomadic feet
Days gone by she trusted him
Opening her soul nightly receiving him
But in the end she was to learn that
    love, like Truth, has no versions
That everything she ever felt was

C. L. Brown

    built atop loose-grained sands,
    and the waves had finally come
That the lies he told to mend those aged
    wounds were actually eating away
    at the calluses she'd form from the repeated
    beatings he broke her with in the first place
That time had finally closed the window
    she found her freedom in
And there she was,
    staring back at the faces mocking her regression
    to the place her tongue condemned the sanctity
    of her very own soul
But tossing stones in her house of
    unfamiliar reflections,
    she finally found the courage
    to shatter the illusions

Bare

Release

One day,
    much like today,
    only not the same
I'll finally put a cutter to your chains in spite
    of my yearning to remain captive
    of the love you don't feel for me anymore

One night,
    much like the one we had our last fight
I will stand,
    my soul unclothed leaving your stains
    to the midnight rain

I will scrub at every print your fingers left in my skin
    when love seemed a permanent thing,
    and your lips spoke the prettiest things
Every memory of every word you've ever spoken
    I'll set to the flame you ignited inside my chest

Then will you read in the smoke
    the tale of destruction you wrote inside my soul,
    and know that you no longer have
    a place inside my void

C. L. Brown

One Mile

One mile,
    14 cryptic scripted words
    spoken from a heart
    at its inception of being broken,
    and their world was never the same
Backtracking unspoken thoughts
    written in the night,
    shedding light,
    he made matters worse
    trying to make it right
    just to prove he was right,
    but he foolishly opened
    the floodgates in her eyes;
    forgetting he knew not how to swim
One mile,
    now each night he relives it all again;
    the shattering of her heart with a few words,
    and an inkless pen
    as he traversed unhealthy emotions
    in the dark resentments that poisoned his soul
One mile,
    wishing he had the chance to drive it again;
    those 5 minutes leading up
    to the second he lost his very best friend;
    asking God to grant him again
    the chance to press backspace
    until every angry word he wrote
    was deleted before his rum-smitten
    finger nervously pressed "Send";
    there beneath that crimson light signaling
    him to stop before proceeding to the collision
    his heart was destined to have with her goodbye
Just one mile,
    that's all it took;
    now he spends nights

Bare

    immortalizing her in his book;
    scripting apologies
    between despondent metaphors and similes
But in all the infinite ways he could ever
    express he's deeply sorry,
    and with all the sincerity he could say,
    "Baby I was angry"
That one mile serves as a constant reminder
    that the heart is best served sharing love
    than it is trying to find ways
    to rewind the passing of times
    it took for granted

C. L. Brown

Unhindered

She said I love you
She said I love you so so so very much
She said I would give my life,
    for you,
    and all you have to do to have it,
    is ask me
She said there were nights
    when I watched you sleeping,
    battling your demons
Some nights when the nightmares were
    too much to bear,
    I watched lukewarm tears
    pouring from your eyes
I just sat there in silence,
    and I wiped them,
    she said
She said I remember one night
    while dreaming,
    you began violently shaking
I tried to wake you,
    but no matter what I did my Darling,
    your soul was in so much turmoil
You wouldn't come back to me
She said, I held you,
    and you shook in my arms,
    and my entire body shook
She said we shook
    as it were the earth cried beneath the deep,
    swaying beneath our feet
We were in complete unison
We had one vibration
She said, I wanted so desperately
    to enter that nightmare,
    and obliterate whatever it was
    that was imprisoning your peace

Bare

But I spoke love into your ear,
    and I spoke love into your lips, she said
She said, I cried over your face,
    and my tears fell onto your cheeks
    as I poured love into your skin
But you just laid there, shaking
Battling those demons
And no matter what I did,
    I couldn't bring calm to that thief
    that was stealing your peace
She said, I would give everything I have
    in this entire world,
    including my own soul,
    just to see that you have peace,
    because I love you
She said, you have but just one thing to do,
    and that is to look inside my eyes,
    because the day will come
    when I won't be able to speak anymore
She said, the day will come
    when I won't be able to touch you anymore
I won't be able to hug you anymore
I won't be able to kiss you anymore
I won't be able to look into your eyes anymore,
    but I need you to understand that
    when that day comes,
    the love I have for you
    will not be diminished one bit
    just because I'm no longer adorned in flesh
She said, because the day that I met you,
    it was your soul that came, and greeted me
It was your soul that came,
    and placed its arms around me
It was your soul that came, and embraced me
And I knew him before I knew your flesh
And I loved him before I loved your flesh
And that is why until my very last breath,

C. L. Brown

I will speak love into you
I will speak love over you
I will speak love around you,
    because... I love you
She said, I know some days
    you might have doubts in your mind,
    but I need you to understand that
    in this time, and the next time,
    I will love you with every bit of myself
She said, I will do anything in this world
    to show it to you
So ask me for my heart, she said,
    and it is yours
Ask me for my eyes, she said,
    and they are yours
Ask me for my hands, she said,
    and they are yours
Ask me for my feet, she said,
    and they are yours
Ask me for my lips, she said,
    and they are yours
Ask me, for my soul, she said,
    and it is yours
Because I love you,
    so so so so very much

She said I thank God
    for that morning the sun rose,
    when my eyes were opened,
    and your eyes were opened,
    and we ventured out into this cold world
    not knowing where,
    or if,
    or when,
    but just like that... we happened
My eyes saw your soul,
    and my body craved your touch

Bare

And I looked at you as you glanced back at me,
    but you seemed not to understand
    the synergy that was at hand,
    and I wanted so badly to hold your hand,
    because I loved you,
    from the very first time
    I laid my eyes on you
Darling, I love you, she said
So so so so so so, very much
And I need you to understand this
    above all else,
    that in this life, or the next,
    whether in, or out of flesh,
    whether with, or without my sanity,
    I will never ever stop calling your name
I will never ever stop loving your name,
    because it is the only name
    in this entire Creation
    that I will call, and you will answer
And that is why I love you
So so so so, very much, she said
So so so so, so very much, she said

C. L. Brown

Lipstick Apologies

I've tried emptying my soul,
    but there aren't enough tears in this world
I've spent way too many days on my knees,
    searching,
    praying,
    playing victim,
    thinking it'd meet again the woman
    who gave me reasons to love again
But this is our end
So please burn the letters you wrote,
    and I hope choke on the smoke rising
    from the lies etched into those tainted pages
In the meantime,
    I'll free my mind of the patient kisses
    while I wash Maybelline's apologies
    from the bathroom mirrors
And before this poem is done,
    please spare me the bullshit,
    and swallow that serpentine tongue
Keep your "I'm sorry"
It was never able to numb the pain,
    or stop the flow of tears anyway
Least my watering eyes blurred your lips
    before I grew tempted to take another sip
    from that reservoir of poison
    I spent latter days submerging myself in
Sometimes I still taste the days
    before that loathsome night;
    seeing again what I never saw
    since I fell in your eyes,
    and I prayed from ignorant lips,
    "Please God, let this be it"
Now I'm left sniffing fragrant shit
    like blooming Orchids
    at the birth of the first season

Bare

Praying to the same God
    from these same lips
    that night will never live
    to see another day;
    though sadly, tomorrow
    I'll be feeding on the same memory;
    the one of your hands around my soul
    when I saw my truth through your lies
You should know you left me completely broken,
    but time's wings bear remedies for my healing;
    though I've since learned
    that hourglass lies horizontal,
    and her sand still holds some residue
    of the ocean's soul

C. L. Brown

> When you cage a bird, you gain a slave.
> When you furnish a place it will be
> protected, cared for, and provided for,
> you gain a companion.

Bare

Gone Girl

Her curiosity traced the rim of his lips
    reading filthy unspoken secrets
Eternity seemed so miniscule
    as he sunk his fingers in
    leaving DNA evidence
    all over her fragile skin;
    praying, anticipating those sins
    would be forgiven
She began slightly shivering as nervousness set in
    so his tongue began massaging her mind
    as his fingers traversed
    the curvature of her spine
He was in the depths of her broken soul,
    perfecting his patchwork
    as he stitched open insecurities
    reciting dope metaphors and cunning similes
Took two sips of her aged wine
    already slowing his mind,
    and became acquainted
    with every drip of her essence
Her speech became slurred,
    but he was thrilled as she whispered,
    "All of it is yours"
Having loose words in her mouth,
    battling indecision,
    he sat his tongue between her muted lips
    silencing every question that questioned,
    "What are you doing?"

The raindrops against the naked window
    harmonized as she reached
    the climax of the song,
    intensifying his erection with
    her serpent-like tongue
Lightning invaded the unlit room

C. L. Brown

    lighting their secrets
    as though their famished souls needed it;
    her sultry moans hushing the grievous thunder
The friction between their skin,
    and the satin sheet covered with white roses
    and tulips aroused a fragrance in the place they
    spent unending minutes
    feasting on wine-soaked skin,
    listening to Passenger's
    fingers plucking guitar strings,
    setting young hearts on fire
That night he burned for her;
    poetry rising from his flames
    because he met death in her eyes,
    and bargained his soul
But as the sun rose,
    she took pieces of his pieces
    and journeyed back home;
    leaving him with sadness, and memories;
    meandering his way through her memories,
    completely alone

Bare

Empty Pages

Darling, I understand
It's difficult making this decision
You're immured by the illusory blue skies
    trapped in his eyes trying to find freedom
Swooned by the sweet lies in his hands
    stirring familiar emotions
There's deadly potion concealed
    behind those flattering lips,
    and he wasted no time casting spells;
    now like heavy grey clouds,
    you're freely falling again
But this stranger in your heart, it's not him
Remember he painted dreams you believed in?
Pretty words, butterflies, and third eye kisses
Now he fakes love raping your soul,
    seeding resentments that will never allow you
    the freedom to forget him
Thumbing through you as he pleases,
    and still hasn't broken the sacred seal
    to your empty pages
Now you move forward in slow motion
    pretending as hard you can,
    but he no longer stands the man
    manning your insecurities;
    hence the tear-soaked sheets
    as you released pent-up emotions
    seeking comfort in fetal positions
His fingers are stranger to your skin
    than the summer sun in the Soul of Winter
You're searching,
    but refuse to acknowledge the fact that
    the love you need reciprocated is missing
Prolonging your breaking heart,
    seeking valid reasons to love him;
    though you know he doesn't deserve

C. L. Brown

the anger that burns within
    each time he takes one more piece
    of the soul breaking beneath his dominance
Tell me, will you realize your worth
    before you become synonymous with his dirt?
Must he say it with a song
    for you to know the thrill is gone?
I know, the way forward seems lonely,
    and unfamiliar
I know you fear starting over,
    but though the past was sweet,
    the present is no less toxic
Darling, there is no light to be had
    in this darkness
And aren't you tired of trying to feel
    your way through the madness?
These words, this poem, it is not meant
    to make your decision
My only hope is that you'll see that
    you'll forever walk blind
    behind a man who lacks vision

Bare

> The journey to finding yourself sometimes
> require that you pass through places
> completely unfamiliar, because sometimes
> to hear your calling, you have to rid
> yourself of familiar noise.

C. L. Brown

Baggage

Neatly she packed all the things she didn't want
    in a beaten-up brown suitcase
    standing lopsided from the missing leg
    that took her balance
Tears poured from both eyes,
    and her nostrils wouldn't have them
    to lament all alone
Her silence filled the vacancy
    of his dreadfully humid bedroom
It was 3:49 on the first side of the day's dawn,
    as images of her smile seeped into
    his conscious mind like sand
    pouring through an Hour Glass
He watched her packing,
    relieving herself of rhetorical questions;
    casting shadows on the naked walls
    they once etched sensual feelings
She carefully laid resentments,
    then neatly placed anger in the upper right corner
Jealousy was next
    being tucked beneath the "Good Morning!"
    texts he would never read again
Tear-soaked insecurities she rolled between the
    sheets of memories they made perfect love in
Then she made room for the pieces
    of her soul that shattered beneath
    the words he spoke when fear got the best of him
That's when it began;
    the commencement of the feelings
    that left him feeling completely empty;
    sitting there wide eyed looking,
    but pride was no longer resident in his eyes
He asked for a last taste of her lips,
    but she refused to unpack it
He asked for her arms around him once more,

Bare

    but those were already at the bottom;
    buried beneath the lies that drove the
    nails in the coffin the night her heart
    was finally broken
She was all done with but a few words spoken
He said, "I love you baby"
She said,
    "Keep it. You'll need it.
    If fact, take mine.
    I don't want it."
It was 4:15 as he woke from his dream
    facing the most hellish reality
Her suitcase was at capacity,
    completely empty
She stood there looking, but not searching
    the void that bore his name
Because the man she knew, and that Soul Breaker
    was certainly not the same
She said,
    "Well that's it.
    I have nothing left.
    Take good care of yourself."
Then she left vacancy in his humid room
    wearing a strapless white dress
    with all she had left;
    purse in her right hand,
    keys in the left
The lopsided beaten-up brown suitcase
    fighting to stand upright as she made
    her way gallantly fading like the darkness
    of the night
Smaller and smaller the cold droplets of tears
    became leaving tracks behind
A sign that in time
    the Hour Glass will collect every grain of
    pain he poured into her soul;
    giving her plenty room to start again

C. L. Brown

> Death was freedom pounding against her skin. Fear was the illusion of a thousand latches giving her reason not to open. But at the voice of Love, wings she grew.

Bare

At the Voice of Love
(For Grandma "Mama")

I have watched helplessly the selfish loitering of time
In silence, my mind flooded with thoughts
    igniting the flame that scorched my broken heart
Laying flowers on your coffin,
    marking with life the place
    death shall keep you bound
Because though time gives us everything,
    eventually,
    in her own time,
    she takes back everything
And now for whatever reason,
    she has taken another of my darlings
But I tried slowing her laboring hand
    perpetuating the memory of your hands
    mending the cracks in my fragile skin
Such a fruitless endeavor
Mama when in a dream I saw your window closing,
    pretending to understand,
    on knees bent I whispered to God,
  "If it's your will"
Self-deception
Because now with tears,
    I am compelled to use this pen
    scripting words my lips didn't get the chance
    to speak into the light of your soul
So now I speak into the darkness
    shedding this light
    knowing that in God you've already won the fight
But this slow creep of time has got me thinking back
    on those times your smile shone
    through the darkened fabric of our souls
It feels so cold standing outside of the darkness,
    because though we are beneath the new sun
    on this new day

C. L. Brown

    we are left to face tomorrow without you
So here we go again
    wiping tears again,
    pouring from our souls again,
    weakened yet again
But you, my sweet Darling,
    had a strength I couldn't fathom
How gracefully you rose from the bottom
    amidst slander, and mockery
    paving your way through eternity,
    making this journey incredibly easier
    for the heirs of your legacy
I remember when last I saw you,
    before your freedom's journey,
    you were the embodiment of strength,
    but fatigue rested in your eyes
    as the leaf nestled in the dirt
    having sheltered her fruit
    to the fulfilment of purpose
So as that leaf Mama, rest now
It is time you sleep now
Your faithful work is over
Because as best as I can remember
    from the dawn of my time,
    til this late November;
    yours was a love that liberated the hearts
    of so many broken
You were a song sung from the very lips of God
A song we sung without the clarity
    of divine understanding
A melody bellowing through the garden of souls
    you tended all of your days

Mama your love was a towering beacon of light
    manning our often tumultuous ocean,
    beaming against the cold dark fears
    of the lost and forsaken

Bare

A sure sign on the uncertain shore
    where we ran bearing tremendous burdens

You were the foundation of this family
The root of something strong, fruitful,
    and so beautiful
So all of our thanks go to you
For the words poured from your lips were
    as fresh waters departing mighty mountains
Replenishing us when courage was a strange thing
But now here we stand on the cusp of death,
    because having nothing left,
    you've chosen to return to God
    his gift of divine breath
So we come now to celebrate the freedom
    of your spirit returning your temple to God's dust
Because you see Mama, death was only freedom
    pounding against your skin
Fear was the illusion of a thousand latches
    giving you reason not to open
But at the voice of love, wings you grew

C. L. Brown

You Deserve

It is evident fear took permanent residency
    in your vacancy
I can feel it in the reluctance your hands manifest
    each time you hesitantly place them on my skin
I know there seem pieces missing,
    and as far as time is concerned,
    it appears you will never mend
I know the words he spoke has got you convinced
    that what you see in that marred mirror
    called self-image is not enough
    to complete the picture
    that speaks of the amazingly beautiful
    being that you are
I know you speak through tears,
    and believe me Beautiful,
    I hear every single packet of air
    that escapes your tired soul
I know when the world grows silent
    the mind shouts in the hollows of your inner-self,
    feeding on the noise reverberating back
    confirming the fact that you are completely alone
Asking, "Why me?"
Staring at yourself choosing only to see
    what he perceived as ugly
You're in his company feeling completely lonely
Wanting to love,
    to be loved,
    but so fearful,
    though she does not abide the latter
But hear these words,
    and listen to the confessions of this heart
    that keeps my life
You deserve the purest love!
Not just the kind he forges
    when the sway in your hips

Bare

    make it hard caging feelings
You deserve the purest love!
Not just the lust in his eyes
    when your body starts submitting to sensual lies
You deserve the purest love!
Not just the illusion of satisfaction
    you fabricate losing yourself in his hands,
    because he craves the taste of your complexion
You deserve the purest love!
The kind that will make you forget
    every single time he's ever opened his mouth
    to break you
But you have to believe that you deserve it,
    then you have to give it to yourself,
    because you are absolutely worth it

C. L. Brown

Recollection

In the shadows I am
Seeking refuge from the star burning
    in the center of my system
I'm making cycles around memories of her
Falling against my will into the centripetal force
    exerted by images of the nights we experienced
    out of body existence inside each other
It's dark here, but I'm home
The distant song of the glad-hearted Nightingale
    conjures thoughts of better days
The child-like nature of the wind romping on my skin
I slow my breathing
Watching sweat beads falling from my eyelashes
    like the heaviness of dark clouds
    when parched ground begs for mercy
I thirst for her gentle arms around me
For the way she used to hold me when our
    hearts found a hiding place from everything;
    sunk deep inside the comfort of that old couch,
    our hearts slowed to the melody of
    Accidental Babies
I've been fighting to avoid these feelings
But this pain in my core keeps finding the cracks
    in my soul
Spewing raw feelings into half-written poems
    between shots of dark rum
Wondering with every tick of that thundering clock
    if she actually misses me
The house's silence amplifies the mockery
    of gleeful orchids hanging from accent walls
Red wine slowing time while I chase tomorrow
    hoping these memories will be gone by then

Bare

> You don't need haters in your life to validate your success, so stop claiming to have them when you don't. Even if you do, you'd be wise not to speak so much of them, because when you speak of them, you give them a voice in your campaign of triumph.

C. L. Brown

Tonight

Tonight, I only wish
To strip you bare
That my ear can make love to your secrets

Tonight, I only wish
To lie next to you
My heart completely nude
That you may see
Just how deeply my pieces adore you

Tonight, I only wish
You'll be completely hushed
That you may taste every single thing
    that breaks my lips,
      receiving every letter of every word
      as I invade your familiar world

Tonight, I only wish
To meet you beneath my darkness
That I may render my eyes completely useless,
    birthing purpose in my lips,
      taking your soul betwixt this life, and the next

Tonight, I only wish
Your gorgeous skin to caress
Massaging poetry like sensual aroma's therapy
    into your flawlessness
To watch the calm in your eyes release my
    unwanted stress

Tonight, I only wish
That you understand I AM your man
The one to be your strength
    when all that you have is gone

Bare

Tonight, I only wish
To dance with your soul
Finding everything I need
    within the simplicity of its music
To kiss it with patience
    while I touch it with purpose

C. L. Brown

> Your eyes tell me your soul is broken, because your yesterday wasn't the best day. But, can I tell you, I've seen your tomorrow, and all I can say is... God is still very much in love with you.

Bare

Birth of Transitional Coupling

The black sun rose in the sunset of her womb,
    narrating the stillbirth of Truth
With poetic words he vividly paint the portrait
    of her unborn self
His black pen oozing black ink
    suffusing her snow-white paper,
    scripting lies for the feast to come
He was there again, bearing fruit of confusion
Giving time reason to pour libation
    to the ghost with the crisscrossed footprints
    leaving tracks in her salt-washed soul
With her bare feet carefully placed inside them,
    she traced the steps death left,
    though her feet were too small to get a true
    sense of the monster lurking in her innocence
With ease he eroded the lies she purposely placed
    revealing deeper feelings,
    but lacked the courage needed
    to reach the depth where silence
    is no respecter of persons
Still his glimmer at her dwelling's surface
    bred hope in her darkness,
    because she gave no purpose
    to those brilliant eyes;
Feasting on regurgitated emotions,
    she ingested his theory
    convincing herself she felt life
But how beautiful the onset of
    the conspiracy of death
But sweet were those dreams of the hereafter,
    and he wasted no time at the table of flesh;
    swaddling her undiscovered days in the past
    where empty promises played dangerous games,
    and pain fell like torrential rain on
    Saharan summer days

C. L. Brown

> Don't waste time thinking about them. If they walked away from your love, they don't deserve your pain.

Bare

Someone Loves You

You wear that fear
   like some priceless garment
Smiling so brilliantly for the blind,
     but I can see clearly inside the caged bird
     silently cries freedom
Here I am breaking my fists against
     metal bars that do not exist
Tears washing the calm from my otherwise
     peaceful eyes, because I can see through
     your false sense of security
I can read every ugly thing you wrote
     believing what that god-forsaken mirror
     whispered to you
But look at me
Look beyond my eyes,
     and see that place
     I have hidden within,
     waiting for you
Everything in, and about me desires
     to love you back to your healing
But you break my heart each time
     you brush my hands away
Still I am here,
     waiting on your heart's waiting to receive
     the love mine was created to give

C. L. Brown

Goodbye Road

Blanket Goodbye Road with the ash
    of the feral flame that we were
A fitting path for this dark heart of mine
    sculpted from her dispirited soul
She was iridescent silver
    swathing the complete moon
But her light is useless
    now that love has set deep roots
    inside the fissures of my fractured soul
My fragile heart bears wounds
    the shape of her toxic tongue
The window of freedom is stained with sorrows,
    and I am the caged bird
    dreaming of unclipped wings
    and the unblemished sun
Some nights I sit the victim of my dying heart
    piping melancholic melodies
    as I intercede, confessing unpardonable deeds,
    because I feel the seductive breath of death
    on the sensitive side of my neck
Some nights he whispers words she once spoke,
    giving me reasons to surrender
One night I remember screaming
    at the top my lungs,
    "I have nothing left for you old friend.
    She took everything."
That night death walked away
    with hands as empty as this
    calloused heart beating in my chest
Some nights I imagine the divine feeling
    of stroking the soft soul of Freedom,
    but I've grown enamored with the prison
    that is her skin;
    lost in last evening,
    fruitlessly trying to snare the setting sun

Bare

But the wind is still so pretty
    kissing her squinted eyes
Time is still so gracious
    persisting her unforgettable smile
My soul is still so frightened growing cold,
    hopelessly screaming "Hello"
    on this Goodbye Road

C. L. Brown

> They watch her in her stride. Walking chin up, face gleaming with pride. They call her names to distract her soul, but she doesn't fit the molds built by simple minds. She is that woman they can't define. So, they shout things seeking her attention; calling her every name beneath the sun, all except the one God spoke the moment He mastered perfection.

Bare

Woman of Shame

Some say her soul God casted
    from the lightless womb
    of an unholy night
A cursed thing whose shame
    is the craftsmanship of the sun;
    though he reveals the divine blessing
    of the essence they sprouted from
Some others say her rich blessing of melanin
    is her suffering depicted
    on the marred canvas time past up
    creating her magnum opus
Some others, spellbound by ignorance,
    claim she's not even worthy of affection,
    yet take pleasure savoring the sweet nectar
    of her divine flower; committing sins
    to the damnation of their wretched souls

But she is the incubator of strength
But she is... the soul of earth
    bearing the complexion of fertile soil
With his best effort, the regal sun took deep
    breaths, and yet couldn't compose anything
    more than a synopsis of her unfathomable
    depths
But she is his Darling
The first fruit of sacred consummation
Her divine womb incubated the brilliant moon
I see pain beautifully depicted
    in her melanated skin
She is sweet manna blanketing their road
    to restoration
But in ignorance,
    blind hands cast stones
    at the birth of redemption

C. L. Brown

One Man's Trash

You keep trying to fix broken promises
    with empty kisses,
    ignoring the tears that
    aren't falling from her eyes
Do you not know her poetry is divine artistry?
God's signature style how He carved her smile
    from the most undefiled thought
Her finer-than-silk mocha skin is the one thing
    I'm willing to die living for
That's why I spend time knees committed to
    floors as I kneel before her altar,
    sacrificing every unhealthy thought
    that represses my consciousness
    of the sacredness that is her
I swear on Heaven,
    Hell envies her fire,
    because my soul still smokes,
    and I'm still a sinner
But am I not a better man for it?
Judge me you will,
    but you haven't laid parched lips against her
    unclothed body though she's spent countless
    days in your frigid company
But believe me,
    eventually she'll lose muscle memory,
    and her hands will forget your skin was ever there

Bare

Sinner

Baptized in this life of sin
Innocence streaming,
    leaving like the sacredness of defiled virgins
Tongue smiting her naked provision
This hallowed offering lying in eager arms,
    but I am the one seeking forgiveness
Fingers gliding, inciting passion
    over nervous skin as poetic excellence
    bring cessation to involuntary respiratory cycles
Lips searching uncovered breasts
    reveling in the freedom of pent-up stress
Cotton sheets firmly clinched
    between pearl-white teeth
Bite marks covering erected tips revealing places
    I freed guarded secrets...
Breathe Darling
Let me take you into the black mind
    saturated with subconscious illusions;
    where untamed thoughts penetrating
    curiosity redefines the notion of intrusion
I am into you, deeply!
Silhouettes of sweet words spoken
    into candles' flames were destined souls burning
    like Hell's fire
Feasting on your nude desire
Depleting everything that makes me who I AM
Replenishing your land as decreed by the great I AM
Reiterating unholy scriptures hoping somewhere
    in this cycle of death's disciples
    I'd meet life,
    and fall deeply into her love again
Going low sacrificing,
    atoning for sin,
    losing the protection of Truth's covering
Completely bare cleansing my skin

C. L. Brown

    only to reveal the stains of her sin
Convincing myself snow will blanket my soul
    the day He calls me home
The ravenous wolf clothed with deception
But breathe, my Darling
Release that poison trapped inside your silence
Baptize me in your freedom
    redeeming in parts my essence
    as I dive soul first into your being
Let me be one with your death
    as you pull life in the updraft;
    depositing transgressions,
    descending into my possession
Both of us physically rising
    though spiritually sinking
Naked as twin fetuses swimming in black sheets
    of seductive passion
So say your last words to the last me
    encased in this snow-painted casket
Drenched in the spit-sprinkled words
    of the preacher man polluting the pulpit
    with white lies as she cries for the old me
    she found in the old days
My face fixed forward staring death
    in his soulless eyes because I see in this end
    the resurrection of the divine self
But am I not the sinner dismissing her
    implicit pleas to bring cessation
    to this divisive mission?

Bare

> There are certain things that defy logic.
> They render the mind useless. But they
> have this beautiful way of reverberating
> inside the soul until your mind decides to
> exercise wisdom, and pay attention.
> Then just like that,
> magic!

C. L. Brown

Misplaced

There was something...
Something beautifully seducing
    about her defeated eyes in the way they took
    shelter behind her untamed hair
The way the smoke lines around them
    streamed sorrows down her saintly face
Against better judgment,
    I was defiantly trying to piece together the story
Trying to rewrite the missing pages
    partially ripped from her unread book
It was then I saw the captive butterfly
    seeking freedom in her despondent eyes
She was gazing sideways at me,
    shielding herself behind obvious fears,
    but the wind,
    having one purpose with my will,
    played gently with her tightly curled hair
And there they were,
    the track marks of pain he graffitied
    all over her purity
But she was beautiful,
    and I fell in love with the mess
    that bore her name
And because she was perfectly broken,
    I paved pathways with beautiful poetry
        to keep her feet above the sewage he left her in
The Art of Fear
    when bruised egos turn bleached canvases
    into dark masterpieces
I found pieces of her peace
    in her counterfeit smile
    as she tried disguising her desperate pleas
And I kissed her...
I kissed her redeeming her soul
    from the hellish memories

Bare

    that refused to set her free
And love,
    she wasn't even guiding me
Yet somehow I managed to traverse
    the intricate pathways
    her pieces were scattered on,
    having big enough hands,
    and a patient enough heart
And love,
    she wasn't even guiding me

C. L. Brown

> Sometimes the favor of God will take you to the top of that mountain concealing your blessing, allowing you to see what He's getting ready to do. If you're ever so blessed, don't let patience be distanced from you. For from the smallest to the mightiest of us, patience is a necessary ingredient in the fulfilment of purpose.

Bare

~~It's~~ Stranger Inside

And then there are those days
    when I seal my lips,
    and I dive deeper into the silence
    of the unexplored pleasures of myself
Some days I reach depths
    that remove purpose from my eyes,
    and it feels like I'm dying
    until suddenly I'll realize
    I feel so much more alive
I see things I can't describe
I hear things I can't repeat
And I perceive that inside I'm a stranger
And it gets me every single time,
    this piece of God inside me I can't deny
Some days I want to take you there,
    but your lips are always moving,
    and your eyes don't always see
    the individual colors that form the rainbow
Sometimes when I'm there I do think of you,
    but only for a second,
    maybe two;
    because your vibration distorts my meditation

C. L. Brown

> I think the collective human spirit is a beautiful enigma. It is a beacon of love. It is a tower of strength. It is a wellspring of hope. It is a flower that has bloomed time and time again in the wake of the mightiest of storms, but I am not at all surprised. After all, it was fashioned in the likeness of the everlasting God, and that is something worthy of praise.

Bare

I Wrote This for You

Death failed to incite fear after I told him
    what I saw in your eyes
Heaven, trying to woo me, fell into a frenzy after
    feeling what I felt when your skin grazed me
I feel no passion when those prior to your entrance
    steal time from my mind
I look to the future where you aren't mine,
    and so realized eventually death pens the story
Baby I love you with a love that has no place, or time
A love I cannot possibly chronicle with this pen
    telling this paper precious secrets
Just thinking of you induces a sense of
    calm so deep inside of me,
        I'd need a thousand do overs at life
        just to begin to comprehend it
And amazingly...
Amazingly, you manage to complete me,
    and I don't even the texture of your name
    leaving my tongue
I'm not familiar with either the pattern,
    or the color of your Iris
I'm not familiar with neither the shape,
    or flavor of your lips
The feel of your skin is entirely foreign,
    and yet I know you better than I do myself
The nights are sick of the routine,
    me on my knees,
    God in my prayers,
    and your name departing my lips
The days?
Yeah, pretty much the same thing
Just go back 5 lines, and read it all again
Even now I am here beneath the complete moon,
    and all I am thinking of, is you

C. L. Brown

> …Like no matter how many times you've seen that person, spanning years even, pretty much every single time you see them there is still some excitement. Every time you make love you touch them like it's the first time; like you're hungry, and all there is to eat is buried inside their soul, so you scratch at their skin as though you're trying to reach life.

Bare

My Beloved

I was a mountain's crest
    aloft cotton fields of snow-clouds
Whispering heartbroken tunes
    in the hasteful wind passing through,
    and around the emptiness that bore my name
Then in my darkness,
    when the lights evaded me,
    my prison's chains fell victim to the monster
    behind the silence in her eyes
She aroused dormant passions,
    coalescing her essence within my quietude
Time was a solitary grain
    of the ocean's playground tossed
    in the angry breeze as I fletcherized
    every definable inch of her ambrosial skin
Shrouding her beautiful within the passionately
    unhurried kisses given
Sacrificing pieces of my broken mess
    one after the next until her soul was
    synonymous with completeness
Even the shadows of curves casted
    when the sun found a place against her skin
    was a delight worth dying for
She was my goddess in a dream
    as my lips worshipped her saccharine covering
Thus slept I the expanse of days,
    lurking in the soul of countless nights
    until my hallucinations of Heaven laid
    as an unborn child in the arms where
    lonesomeness thrived in the memory
    of former days

C. L. Brown

> And sometimes you just need to release deep inside of her. To get messy. To get intimate. Damn near gasping for air trying to let it all out. Telling her things only God knows; learning things you must swear never to repeat. Right there on the couch, ignoring friction inducing distractions like notification vibrations, experiencing multiple mindgasms through soul-bending conversations.

Bare

Complete Moons, and Star Dusted Skies

May I pass time inside of you?
Out where complete moons, and star dusted skies
    take pleasure in words that
    describe love's breathtaking soul?
May I lay me down in your silence?
Out where jealousy's lips are muted?
Out where anger is not acquainted
    with our hearts?
Out where my eyes lose purpose,
    that I may see the beautiful scars
    decorating your gorgeous soul?

May I pass time inside of you?
May I share the prettiest words I can find,
    and tell you exactly how ugly this life is
    outside of you?
May I give you reasons to smile
    as time ages outside of us?
May I place what I've seen inside your soul
    in this book so that the Universe may
    witness the unseen beauty of our Creator
    through these awestruck eyes of mine?
May I give you everything I'm not,
    so you'll have the very best of me?

Do you know, should death whisper your name
    I'd answer in your stead?
Do you know, should Heaven deny you rest,
    I'd walk the unending path of death
    right there next to you
Do you know what comes after you?
Nothing!
Where you stop, is where I end
That's where life itself ends
Do you know how much I crave you?

C. L. Brown

Do you know some days when I pull you in
    I'm really trying to fit myself between
    your soul and your skin
Futile I know,
    but one day,
    my will will make this way out where
    complete moons, and star dusted skies
    take sweet pleasure in the breathtaking view
    of your astonishing soul

Bare

> It's quite simple. I chose to believe in those who believed in me until I learned to believe in myself.

C. L. Brown

God's Prettiest Thought

She is, the manifestation
    of God's prettiest thought
Skin like sunburnt clouds
    when I bury my face between her breasts
    breathing miracles to my new-found self
She is, the manifestation
    of God's prettiest thought
Lips like rain-soaked cotton tasting my skin
    revealing secrets like receding seas
    before the deluge comes
    replenishing parched sand
She is, the manifestation of
    God's prettiest thought
Eyes the color of Manuka Honey possessing my soul
    like those earthbound angels of old
She is, the manifestation
    of God's prettiest thought
Voice like Chopin's fingers
    striking white between black keys,
    playing my flat lined song
    unto my soul's redemption
She is, the manifestation
    of God's prettiest thought
Tongue mastering alchemy
    making truth of the lies imprisoning me
She is, the manifestation
    of God's prettiest thought

Bare

> I ingested her ghost like Cuban smoke
> knowing it was poison. But how sweetly
> she soothed me as I stripped bare the
> memories of all the pain.

C. L. Brown

Purgatory

She was poison!
She was medicine!
She was poison!
She was medicine!
She was poison!
She was medicine!
She was medicine!
She was poison!
She was... poison!
She was... medicine!
And I lived
And I died
Inside of her
And as the Grim Reaper's wintry fingers
    unhurriedly inched themselves deeper inside
    my consciousness
And the subtle beats of my heart became
    the sounds of distant drums
    making eventual requests
    of the generous wind
I reached into the Most Holy
    of the Divine Being,
    receiving just a hint of all that she was to me
It was in complete blindness
    that I grazed her face becoming acquainted
    with the joy, and the pain
    that spoke of the beauty, and the blemishes
    of her alluringly cherubic charm
But she allowed me... to live!
In a split second
And all of my years upon this earth
    could not stand in comparison
I perished inside of her that night
And when I made it to the other side of death
    death looked at me,

Bare

    but he saw her
He saw how beautiful she was
He saw how divine she was
He saw how perfect she was
And death could not get his frigidly dark hands
    around her body of pure light
So death passed over,
    because I was her,
    and she was me
And so I lived
But I am not so certain
    that I am happy to be here
Because what I experienced inside
    her darkness that night...
    I have never seen such light
I have spent years trying to live,
    but found the essence of life in a split second;
    when all that I was flashed
    in the depths of her eyes,
    as she administered her medicine
    in a tiny dose of pain

C. L. Brown

Former Things

I apprised her I was no angel,
    but should truth be told,
    I lacked all resemblance of her demons
Still poison dripped from my lips
    like legions of those fallen ones,
    because I was delighted having
    sight of His creation
She had no eyes for my Light,
    so I spoke confusion
Watching my tongue creeping down her abdomen,
    springing tributaries of emotions
    that converged into her ocean,
    and I was the river sprung at the apex
    of her lower self,
    emptying my cares into her depths;
    indulging in seductively sweaty sex
Faith was no missing ingredient,
    but I had no taste for her surface,
    so I allowed myself to slip beneath her waters,
    waiting patiently to receive
    mouth to skin resuscitation
Watching her falling into her out of body experience
She fell into a trance at the onset of levitation,
    thighs straddling my neck as she opened up
    to receive the words my tongue used
    to draw her waters;
    the exhibition of her satisfaction seeping through
    disintegrated fingers
She advised me she'd spent former days
    hoping he'd express regret
Her heart trying to peruse the cryptic codes
    pulsating from her soul when he abused her body,
    but couldn't induce a slight climax in her mind
So I assured her from behind,
    those days were now behind

Bare

> You cannot give reverence to the rainbow when you despise its colors. In the same light, you cannot truly revere God when you detest the things of God.

C. L. Brown

Between the Rains

We laid beneath the
    silhouetted patterns of inquisitive palm trees;
    wedged between the recesses
    of Floridian rains
The soft wind carried Golay's guitar's strings
    strumming streams of dreams,
    inseminating the poem I manifested her in
I watched the starving wrinkles crisscrossing
    my aging skin frowning,
    because my hands crave the feel
    of the cotton-like clouds God concealed
    her essence with
My pen culminating her poem's gestation
    traced the sexy exuded from her
    protruded hip, allowing me a sip
    of the sacred waters prostrated
    before the throne of the One everlasting
I was saturated in the precipitation
    of her beautiful;
    finding myself again in the finesse of God's
    fingers as she patched my fractured pieces
    with that smile that always
    rendered me new
And how I envied the morning's eye rising,
    lighting the parts of her grace
    not intimate with the lustful thoughts
    ascending from the ancient deep
I even envied the eastbound earthbound wind
    invading her supernal skin
In my mind my tongue searched
    the shadows revealing
    the parts of her sensual art
    the partially sighted sun had not visited
And I was confused why the ocean
    she was submerged in had not swallowed up

Bare

    every drip of her naked truth
But I was pleased to see some residue
    of her ambrosial provision remaining
    for my seraphic lips to feast upon
So I took time between her layers of satisfaction
    slowly sinking my teeth
    into her forbidden fruit,
    ingesting spiritual secrets,
    reliving the shame of man
    in the cool of the day
And though as one who's forfeited his way,
    I discovered my destiny in the hills and valleys
    through which her adventurous curves
    carried me
My God!
You should see the things she showed me,
    there between the rains, as the sun casted
    intricate shadows of the mysteries
    she imparted me
But please,
    allow me to tell you about
    her unparalleled beauty
Her face was the bewitching image of God
    reflecting a network of flaming stars;
    snaring my wandering soul
    as she expanded my consciousness
Her voice was the pitch-perfect masterpiece
    of stringed instruments soothing my demons
Her eyes were falling stars fulfilling
    my unspoken wishes
Her knotted hair swaying like aged trees
    was the playground of the youthful breeze
Her skin tone was the comfort I called home
Her passion was the prison I sentence myself in
    seeking life until I found death,
    and resurrected in the first day of her eternity
Her desires rippled through my placid waters

C. L. Brown

    like boisterous winds grooming the faces
    of sleeping oceans
Her fathomless soul was my ocean,
    and her depth took my last breath
    as I dove deep exposing myself
    to all her possibilities
And so we laid there,
    between the rains,
    while Golay's guitar's strings
    strummed streams of my dreams;
    inseminating this poem
    as my soul immersed itself deeply
    between her waters

Bare

Monologue

I wish to spend days with you
    not counting falling suns,
    or rising moons
Days not putting a thing to my lips except it be
    indistinguishable from the flavor
    of the words rising from the irresistible you
Days where the morning's birds are silenced
    each moment you open your mouth
    to set free the song that keeps your heart
But I haven't the slightest clue who you are
At least physically, not yet
But foolish ole me spend many nights
    kissing your nose then your eyes
That is my silly way of praying that
    you will never lay eyes on those things
    destined to break you

I think mostly of the first day we'll
    ever unify space and time
I think about the colors of your eyes,
    and wonder if they'll match the colors of the sea,
    giving me reasons dive inside them
I think of the fire that will burn within us, through us
I imagine we'll consume everything
    prior to us, until we rise from the remains
    of the past to a future that keeps no memory
    of said days
I yearn to feel the texture of the place on your cheeks
    where my lips will lay claim to them
So I'll make gold of this patience
Just promise me you won't keep me
    waiting until God declares my end
Because frankly, it's tiring
    Entertaining these spiritual strangers

C. L. Brown

> We often hear how much God is a healer, but we sometimes don't realize that God is also a breaker. God will break you! He will allow you to be broken; however, when God breaks you it is not to destroy you; it is to build you back stronger than you've ever been.

Bare

When the World Grows Silent

When the world grows silent,
    and the wind is the voice of God
I listen to the good fortune spoken
    of the time not yet though coming
Then I take on the ways of submissiveness,
    succumbing to the crossing,
        seeking the birth of life away from my lies,
    and the parts of myself I despise
Becoming foolish I grew wise in His eyes
Because the seed bears no fruit lest it dies
So blanket me with the soul of earth
Red dirt, and the residuum of opacus clouds
In time I will break free when the Son returns
    to call forth from darkness the one wilted
    from the sorrows of confinement
Daily I fight seeking freedom,
    constructing the bars of pure fear
    that will eventually keep me bound
Though the sight of the careless wind
    having its way with uncommitted leaves
    is the dream my soul refuses to wake from
His words inside of me is water to desert sand
Seeping through me as water in a child's hand
And all my days I've played the boy
    dying to become the man
To sit at His right hand
Giving up the flesh that I may know the life
    lived before my descent into death
But when He asked for what remained
    I said there's nothing left
Though my heart gave up my secrets
    aching for the one that yesterday left
When I poured out the best of what I had
    convincing myself I wasn't all bad

C. L. Brown

But then I saw in His reflection my painfully
    slow slide to dereliction
Unpardoned sins telling me I'm inferior
    to the love set aside for the ones
    on the narrow path
But here I'll sit till I wither away
    as the time-casted branch,
        and the breeze comes speaking spiritual healing
        against the things of my soul death is stealing
I am taken by the chilling vibration of
    God's voice in this passing wind
Basking in the life He keeps speaking,
    now that my world has grown still

Bare

> Let the Creator know what you want, and work towards it while letting go of how it comes to pass.

C. L. Brown

Futile

She sat out on a course of trampled hearts
Racing time
Hoping that in him she'd find the security
    her heart searches for
But his words are toxins,
    and in his arms death becomes her inheritance
He's spent many days touching her skin,
    but her soul has no prints
So, she's buried herself beneath anger, sadness,
    and resentments,
    knowing he will never see the light
    she is to his misguided intentions
Seeking truth,
    uncovering lies,
    falling victim to seductive persuasion
Even the tears she can't stop crying
    declares just how much she needs distance
Spending countless nights in dark rooms,
    counting down the minutes till morning
    brings him back to the pile of dirt
    he makes of her
But she loves him, foolish the heart
This master manipulator,
    a traitor to the soul who wants nothing
    more than to die living for him
This Alchemist receiving gold,
    contriving washed out silver

Bare

> When the Sheppard wrestles with the
> sheep, wolves dine on the flesh of kings.

C. L. Brown

Dust

Where am I going?
Is there a place for me?
Do you not see?
I AM nothing
Yet everything
An easy burden for the still soft wind
Shifting from death to life then back again
Having mastered both from the beginning of my end

Where am I going?
Is there a place for me?
A place for my pain?
For my truth?
For my emptiness?
I have given you all that I AM
But you are not satisfied
See how you sift me apart seeking yourself?
I AM you
Can you not see?
Do you not hear my song?
I have given my soul to the wind
    in hopes that in my dying
    you would remember Him
As I pass through time
A void
A blackness
A darkness
An emptiness seeping through the porous nature
    of your carefully woven thoughts
I ate away at you
Now I AM you

See the stars above?
Below?
Within?

Bare

Without?
Where is the beginning?
Where do I end?
How can I master the heavens
    having not mastered my dust?
I
    AM
            the multiplication of stars
My fire endures forever
I purge them preparing for the Savior
I purge them preparing for the Savior
I purge them preparing for the Savior
Completion
Three being One
From nothing
From darkness
From blackness
Now open your heart
Receive the tidings of the still soft wind

C. L. Brown

> Don't ever lose sight of yourself, and your values in the options they present you with. Choosing none is also a valid choice, so don't be afraid to walk away with D, *None of the above.*

Bare

Restoration

The sun is black,
    and you took my moon
She was you
So here I am back in her womb
    waiting to be born
        again,
            to try again,
                finding you

C. L. Brown

> When your wings are ready to withstand the wind, Courage and Faith will provide the perfect balance. So, don't ever be afraid to show those mountains the capabilities of God's hands.

Bare

Open and Shut

She found me rummaging through dated variants
    of my present self
Us both perplexed in light of the version
    chosen to persist
But she opened her eyes
So I opened my heart
Then we loved each other
Swearing we'd never part
But then the war started,
    because we forgot how empty the world was
    before the heavens conspired for us to be
So I looked past her, admiring me
Then I closed my eyes
Having nothing else to see
And it broke her heart
Completely shattering me

C. L. Brown

Soul of Heaven

What is she like,
    this Soul of Heaven?
Are there words worthy of hosting her Truth?
Synonyms that defy
    the antonyms
        proclaiming how beautiful she isn't
Do vapors
    of fallen clouds
        shroud her nakedness?
Shades of white
    amalgamated with tones of gray
        yielding the perfect
            resemblance
                of the
                    unseen God
Is her softness that of the Autumn's mist?
Are there remedies
    fixed between her
        sweeter-than-honey-stained lips?
Do orchids freely grow
    from the rich soil
        of her fertile thoughts?
Do they dance arousing her most beautiful smile?

Do eclipsing moons snare the eyes of her love?
Is freedom conceived in the womb
    of her virginal mind?
Is it sweet to the taste,
    her colorful simplicity?
Do towering strands of feral grass
    romp on her skin in vain?
Do they dance against her covering without purpose?

What is the sound of her silence?
Shhh,

Bare

   with your heart,
      please,
         just listen
Does the wind bearing her secrets
   know the name of her celestial mystery?
Does her tears mollify life's pains
   as the compassion of early spring rains?
Does darkness dare enter her sphere of light?
Does the intruding sun dare walk away
   from the strands of her hair
      stolen by the jealous breeze?

What is her complexion?
Tell me about her complexion
Are there colors in this realm
   so honored to adorn her skin?
Can the adept Cello master her melody?
Can he play her as perfectly
   as the mastery of God finger's
      when they manifested
         His heart's most desired?
What does she feel like,
   this Soul of Heaven?

C. L. Brown

> Describe to me in the finest of details the appearance of the fish, and I will show you the image of God.

Bare

God of Wonders

Listen!
Careless children
Just listen
Do you hear it?
Set your heart against the wind, and listen
Do you not hear it?
Do you not feel it consuming your being
    like an untamed flame preparing the
    sterile ground for new birth?
The quiet prayers of the Whistling-pine
The supernal voices of those fallen
    not familiar with death
Sweet aromas of praise ascending from sacred lips
The Bluebird's blues
The Lion's thanksgiving for
    the Everlasting's provisions
The ant's dance for the returning rains
Shades of the wind mirroring the hues
    of the water's bow
Restless waves going to and fro
    removing the outcasts of the sea
The fingers of the new born baby
    clasping the hand of love
Do you not see?
Is this not God?

C. L. Brown

> I burned a forest to the ground, and watched life sprung from the ash. That's when I knew death was only the beginning.

Bare

Fear of Fear

The quiet plea of curiosity
   mixed with the fear resident in your eyes
You're dying to know what it is I feel for you
To know why my chest burns each,
   and every single time that I think of you
But are words so generous?
Suppose I tell you I breathe only
   that I may live for you?
What if I wish greatly to meet you where you
   are most lonely, and spend time in that place
     until you know every single thing about me?
Would you believe if I told you I desire to go
   below your gorgeously colorful layers?
To wipe away the last drop of black tears
   your sweet eyes will ever shed?
To patch every crack that seeps insecurity
   with reassurance
      as I place my lips
         over your guarded skin
           with absolute patience?
What if I am ready to answer every question doubt
   has when you become free beneath my hands,
     and I erase your fears
        with the very essence of man's heart?
What if I wish to kiss your quieted lips
   until they become too pure
     to ever utter a word of bitterness?
What if I wish to wipe from your memory's
   stained pages every ugly thing he's ever spoken
     into your spirit?
To make love to you again and again
   until you bloom in color like the flower
     God kept in mind
        the day he fashioned you?

C. L. Brown

I do!
I wish!
Every single night in fact
But you won't let me
Because you refuse to see past him
    though he's only a Lion's roar
        in a distant shadow
Should it be possible
    I'd rip a whole deep and wide enough
        in this heart of mine,
            and show you the palace I've built
                brick-by-brick for this Queen
                    who's captured my being
But you won't let me
Because no matter how pretty I make you feel
    his refusal to see you still has you
        trying to show him how wonderful
            you already are
                in these doleful eyes of mine
You are still trying to show the blind
    the brilliant star I wished upon
        every time the darkness fell
So now you know
Though the truth is,
    this won't change a thing,
    because you still keep thoughts of him
Still too afraid
To ever let me in

Bare

> New wings glory in faith. Old wings glory in wisdom. Both of these have a place.

C. L. Brown

Shells of Sea's Shore

I've heard fingers stroking piano keys
    trying to play the melody sunflowers dance to
    when midday suns light her face
    showing those dimples
She's absolutely incredible
And I've fallen so deeply inside her
    I can taste her every whisper before
    she's even conscious of them
My worst days are envied by Heaven's best,
    should only I make space for her smile
    in my mind
Have you seen the silvery moon
    rising from the ocean in the reach of your soul?
Have you listened to the stories
    the sea washes ashore?
She's even more breathtaking,
    revealing virginal thoughts,
    allowing me to break her silence
I evade this existence,
    and all its places she isn't found
    when I spend time in her eyes
    in places God alone can see
I pass my fingers against her soul
    manifesting God in all His glory
She wonders if love is my incentive
I suppose she presumes I drive 35.4 miles,
    weakened by the sleep in my eyes,
    simply to count the scattered stars
    of the cloudless night
I have fallen for her
So much deeper than she'll ever know

Bare

> When I was living, I thought about riches.
> Now that I'm dying I think about love. I
> only wish I'd lived for what I'm dying for.

C. L. Brown

Into the Mystic
(Remembering Craigmore & Keroy)

Set free these aged pieces of all that I AM
Let me sit to listen to the guarded secrets
   of the aimless wind
Let me dance among sun-bathed clouds
Let the crowns of mountains
   wash my tear-stained feet,
   for I have known grief
I care not where I am found
   when the Spirit which heals finds me scattered
   across the ageless face of time
For I will be free,
   and freedom is the likeness
   of the unseen certainty of He which has no end
And Freedom, is the sweet song of love
   pacifying the most dreaded of my demons
So when you take thought of me my beautiful friend,
   let not a single tear blur that gorgeous memory
   when my words are no more
   to induce your comfort
But remember the sound of my laughter
Keep to the front of your mind my smile
For these were my remedies,
   and tried I did to heal your broken spirit
So cry if you will,
   but not of grief;
   for I am now comforted
   by the delicate hands of love,
   and she dares to unearth all my possibilities

Bare

> Everything we need for the journey is already on the path. All we have to do is be brave enough, and have enough faith to keep putting one foot in front of the other.

C. L. Brown

Brother's Keeper

It is thunderous whispering in solitude
You find yourself drowning in thoughts
    as the grief spills over onto the paper
    listening beneath your trembling fingers
You're searching early memories for smiles
    to undo the art of death,
    but he's a master at his craft,
    so the tears blur your eyes,
    and all is gone before you wipe the fog away
You find yourself before God
    beneath a mountain of questions
    you don't have the courage to ask
But now and again, "Jesus help!" bellows
    from your numbness,
    shaking the very core of all that you are

But I know the road you walk
I know very well the potholes
    that will leave your ankles fragile
I know where it narrows
I know the place your tears will flow most,
    and when you've arrived,
    you'll find the ground still stained with grief
I know where the sun submits to thick darkness,
    the moon hides her face,
    and the stars decide not to give their light
I know the bitter words that will remain
    lodged in your throat
    as your eyes search the visible world
    for signs of an invisible God

I know the loud voice of loneliness,
    and the doleful song of the clock
    perched on the muted wall,
    slowly reminding you, in time alone

Bare

I know that dreadful stare of fear
    on the faces of those who seek strength
    in your weakness
I know the fruitless search for hope
    in that dying memory you're
    fighting hardest to keep alive
I know the chorus of raindrops
    harmonizing behind your heartfelt solo
But be of good strength,
    for I know the arms of love
    when comfort is her provision;
    for I have seen the darkness bow
    before the radiantly rising sun,
    and I have felt the tender hands of time
    wiping the residue of tears
    I never wanted to cry

C. L. Brown

> I just want a journey with you so incredible
> I wouldn't even attempt it again for fear
> that just one strand of the hair on your
> head wouldn't fall in the same place.

Bare

Her Song, My Love

She has this thing about her that words simply
    can't seem to do justice
The first time I met myself I was somewhere
    lost in her eyes finding directions in her lips
I told her so many times to me she's
    absolutely perfect
I told her she's my end though she has
    a hard time believing this
I told her she's the most beautiful music,
    and that I dance each time she gives me
    the chance to spend time in her mind
She told me once,
    maybe twice,
    that I was a sweetheart
I told her once,
    maybe twice,
    that all the good that I am is but a reflection
    of everything that she is
She asked me once,
    maybe twice,
    what is it you mean by this?
The bee is always most sweet
    around honey, I said,
    so maybe,
    perhaps,
    possibly the good you see in me
    is what you are to me
Maybe,
    perhaps,
    possibly what you feel is the life
    you've gifted me
Maybe,
    perhaps,
    possibly what you hear is the song
    you've written on the tablets of my heart

C. L. Brown

I told her
Darling! I said
I know nothing before you,
    so since you are my start,
    won't you also be my end?
I told her
Darling! you truly are my friend
I told her
Darling, I've tried seeing myself
    taking you out of the picture
But Darling! I said,
    I've never seen anything more broken
    than me without you
I've never seen anything more empty
    than my lips without yours pressed up
    against them
I've never in my life my Darling,
    seen a man more forsaken than what I saw
    that day when my mind took your face
    out of my space

So maybe I AM sweet
Maybe I AM kind
Maybe I AM loving
Maybe I AM your everything
But Darling, the bee is most sweet around honey,
    so please permit me to stay this way
    until my start, and my end
    meet in the very same place

Bare

> No matter how rich the soil a seed is sewn in, it is no guarantee the plant won't wilt beneath the sweltering sun. It is no guarantee storms won't abuse it. It is no guarantee insects, and animals won't feast on its leaves before it bears fruit. But if it endures these things, the day will come when we will know life partaking of its fullness.

C. L. Brown

Bare

I swear on everything that I AM,
    I would still the perpetuation of confusion
    if only for a million lifespans
    compressed into one second,
    that you may understand
    this breathtaking enigma trying to find
    a place inside your emptiness
I've laid bare my soul on lined sheets
    of dead trees trying to find the life
    I was never away from
All to set free myself of that dead stare you keep
    resident in those frigid eyes
You carry questions as expectant women,
    but should answers be now delivered,
    they'd lack the ability to survive outside
    the lies you've grown accustomed to
Still it is quite evident you which to voice them,
    but reasons unknown compel you
    to keep them off your lips
So, I placed mine against your skin in silence,
    quieting my breathing,
    dispelling the obstacle that you were
    to your own self
I saw everything you're hiding from
I was puzzled,
    but I suppose mirrors are pointless
    to those things that render words useless

I've seen time age, but that moment that looked
    upon your face stood still
So I swallowed every word that knew not
    how amazing you actually are,
    trusting the sun's promise to rise

Bare

    in the hour you'll be ready to
    truly see yourself

Last time we met I kissed you with a thought
    that went beyond your flesh
    imparting the flavor of my breaking heart
    to your insensitive soul
You healed it, though selfishly
I've gifted your wings winds of a love
    I haven't given
I've journeyed through those invitingly beautiful
    eyes you see not from,
    and saw God devising the Universe,
    and all its parallels in colors I am forbidden
    to mention
Except how much they exemplify
    your resplendent complexion
I've engrossed you with my expressions of love,
    walked uncharted places of death with you
    falling apart in my careful hands,
    then brought you back in my life to this end
I held you,
    and your fingers' patience paralyzed
    my thinking
So, I closed my eyes purposely passing my face
    against the inside of your hand
And my heart raced
And my belly gave freedom to caterpillars
And you pulled water from my eyes
And I pulled water from your eyes
And you found comfort against my chest
And my words cradled your mind
And your lips forced mine apart
And we departed this dying flesh
And we met in that place adjacent to death,
    where our individuality was sacrificed
    upon the altar of singularity;

C. L. Brown

    where the solitary flame danced in
    solitude to the only song love's ever sung
Where I tried to find separation,
    but you were fused perfectly with perfection
So I laid bare my soul on lined sheets
    of dead trees trying to find the life
    I was never away from
Seeking God, gazing at distant stars
    when all of life's expanse has been right here
    within the reach of my hands
The futile efforts of a man
    seeking freedom outside of wisdom
But I swore on this emptiness I'd still this
    cyclic spin only for you
Only that you may understand the enigma that I AM
Hoping that in the end when
    we can no longer make amends,
    you will see that all along you were me
    trying to find yourself in the stranger
    you've never been away from

Bare

> Consider the Red Wood, how it sweeps the floor of the heavens, yet it remains firmly rooted in the soul of the earth. You would be wise to stay grounded as you soar.

POET. WRITER. INSPIRATION.

A man of purpose whose ambition it is to leave an indelible impression on our world, **C. L. Brown** was born, and raised on the island of Jamaica before migrating to the United States. He also authored the poetry collection *Loud Whispers of Silent Souls*.

For more information, visit www.authorclbrown.com

www.ingramcontent.com/pod-product-compliance
Lightning Source LLC
Chambersburg PA
CBHW020611300426
44113CB00007B/603